24.95

Job Hunting in New York City

2007 Edition

WetFeet Insider Guide

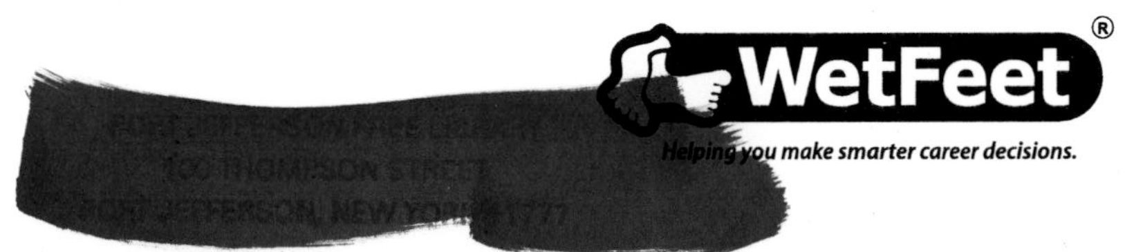

WetFeet, Inc.

The Folger Building
101 Howard Street
Suite 300
San Francisco, CA 94105

Phone: (415) 284-7900 or 1-800-926-4JOB
Fax: (415) 284-7910
Website: www.wetfeet.com

Job Hunting in New York City

2007 Edition
ISBN: 1-58207-688-X

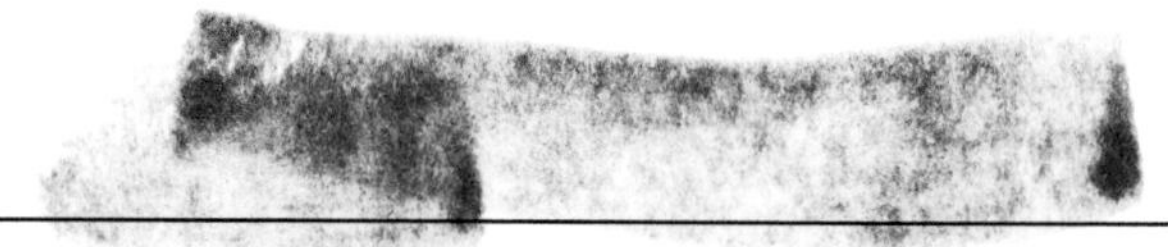

Table of Contents

Job Hunting in New York City at a Glance

The NYC Job Market

- More than eight million people live in greater New York City (1.5 live in Manhattan), and …
- … More commute from Long Island, Westchester County, northeastern New Jersey, and southwestern Connecticut.
- 3.6 million people are employed in New York City (February 2006); two thirds of those jobs are in Manhattan.
- As of February 2006, 213,600 New York City residents were unemployed and actively looking for work. Add in the number of people who are dissatisfied with their jobs and waiting for the right moment to start looking, and you have a large population of job seekers to compete with.
- Nearly every career and every industry in the United States is represented in the New York job market.
- New York City's unemployment is at its lowest rate in five years: 5.5 percent in March 2006 (New York State Department of Labor). Add 10.2 percent to account for the underemployed.
- It's a great time to find a job in New York. Tourism and Wall Street have contributed to a modest job growth in the city and Monster Worldwide reports more jobs posted online in New York than ever before.
- Demand is sharpest for managers, educators, arts and media professionals, physical and social sciences workers, and health care practitioners.

Doing Your Homework

- Like anywhere, the best jobs are found through personal referrals.
- Be proactive about what you want and where you want to work; don't be shy about making it known.
- Look for information on company websites, general classified advertising (either online or in print), industry or association publications and websites, and the career offices of colleges and universities.
- Create a target list of potential employers to keep your job search organized.
- Understand that submitting a resume and cover letter is not enough. Personal contact is key.

According to NYC Job Seekers . . .

A job search in New York City is the same as a job search anywhere—simply multiply by ten.

"Looking for a job is the most difficult thing. But I love New York. It was worth the effort [to relocate and search for a job]."

"Having a contact and a referral makes a difference. It really is about who you know. It's kind of daunting."

"At a minimum, it's good to apply online, but there are so many people that do that, I think it's important to take additional steps to make sure you get called in for an interview."

"The biggest obstacle for me in my job search is overcoming impatience. I have to remind myself that finding the right position takes a marathon, not a sprint. Concentrating on day-to-day accomplishments helps."

Landing Your Dream Job

- Patience and persistence are key. Plan to search for one to two months for every $10,000 in salary.

- A resume alone won't get you a job; nor will an interview. A successful job search requires attention to each step of the effort: developing contacts, conducting research, presenting a strong resume, interviewing, and following up effectively.
- Market yourself the way you would a product or service. Ask yourself, "What's in it for the buyer?"
- Declare yourself. Don't leave an interview without conveying your interest in the job.
- Assess potential employers in the same way they assess you.
- Connect the dots in your interviews and in your cover letters. Don't just tell a reader or interviewer what you did; tell them how it applies to their company and their job.
- Know your value in the marketplace.
- Don't get caught short: Keep your resume up to date—even when you're not looking for work.

The City

Overview

Geographic Considerations

Major Industries

Employment Trends and Outlook

Overview

New York, New York. The Big Apple. If you can make it here, you can make it anywhere.

There's truth to these clichéd phrases. New York City is a $450 billion economy. If it were a country, it would be the tenth largest in the world. Some of the world's largest companies are based here—41 of the Fortune 500—and it's considered the top rung for finance, fashion, publishing, and the arts. Whether you're climbing the ladder toward being the next Donald Trump, Donna Karan, Helen Gurley Brown, or Twyla Tharp, high-profile careers are forged in New York City.

Many people find the prospect of doing business in New York both exciting and intimidating. It's the commerce center for the Western world, where multibillion-dollar deals are made, where the top newscasters give their reports, where Madison Avenue, Wall Street, and the New York Stock Exchange are located, and where the United Nations Security Council meets. Times Square with its flashing video screens is a monument to corporate branding. Even the modest chess club you might walk by in Greenwich Village is famous—it's where world chess champion Bobby Fischer cut his teeth. What you do here counts, whether you spend your day playing chess in the park or making a market for the next Google stock.

But New York is a working town, where slackers need not apply. To be successful in business here, you can't sit back and wait for opportunity to knock on your door. Someone else will have intercepted it on the way over. Successful New York City job seekers exploit every opportunity and aren't shy about asking for contacts and referrals. If this sounds ruthlessly self-serving, you might want to reconsider the idea of living and working here. On the other hand, if you want to land a job in one of the world's most dynamic business environments, then throw a bridle on that fabulous New York energy and get ready for the ride of your life.

A NEW YORK STATE OF MIND

Not only do New Yorkers work hard, they play hard. Home to a vibrant arts scene, the New York Yankees and Mets, film festivals, concerts, restaurants, clubs, courses, lectures, museums, galleries, Central Park, and shopping...well, let's just say there's always something to do. Which is good because you'll live either in quarters the size of a suburbanite's laundry room or with as many roommates as a college student. Whether you're tired of looking at the four walls of your studio or the faces of your roommates, you'll want to get out. The restaurants and shops stay open late most nights to accommodate a long workday.

DON'T BOX YOURSELF IN

Take your job search outside your apartment. Especially if you're accustomed to working in an office environment surrounded by coworkers and the accompanying culture of lunch and coffee dates, you might find it isolating to conduct a search from within the confines of a tiny New York studio apartment. One insider says, "I'm such an extrovert, I thought I was going to go buggy after the first two days at home. And I have an L-shaped studio with an amazing view!" Her solution? "I always have appointments lined up so that I'm out at least once a day, even if it's only for a walk." Others do their Internet research and email work in Starbucks, or the library, and save their phone work for home.

You've probably heard that things move quickly in New York. Watch out on that first day: While you're craning your neck up toward the sparkling spire of the Chrysler Building, your fellow pedestrians are likely to mow you down. Everyone is in a hurry, and nowhere is this more apparent than in the pace set by people on foot. Wait for a walk light? Only if you can't beat the car that's barreling toward you. The light with the flashing hand that signals "wait" is interpreted by New Yorkers to mean "look." If there is no oncoming traffic, the sidewalk crowd doesn't even break stride, flowing around the guy who follows the rules (a sure sign you're from out of town) like water around river rocks.

New York City's legendary high energy hits you like one of its notoriously muggy summer days: It's palpable. If you've come from a place that runs at a slower pace, you might feel that you're falling behind, and that you must work ever harder and longer just to keep up. Pacing yourself is the key. Take a deep breath (but not near that pile of garbage), and tackle first things first. Before you know it, you'll be pushing ahead of the crowd to step into the crosswalk, and your friends back home will remark how quickly you seem to have adopted a New York attitude.

THE CITY AND ITS ENVIRONS

The island of Manhattan that many people think of as New York City is actually the smallest of five boroughs comprising a 314-square-mile area that also includes Brooklyn, Queens, Staten Island, and the Bronx. Greater New York City is home to 8.1 million people, and more commute into Manhattan from Long Island, Westchester County, northeastern New Jersey, and southwestern Connecticut. If you want to feel the full effect of New York's morning rush, stand in Grand Central Station's main terminal any weekday around 9 a.m. to watch a fabulous convergence of blue serge and pinstripes arriving from the wealthy suburbs.

Bounded by the East River, the Hudson River on the west, and joined by the Harlem River at the north, Manhattan is 14 miles long and 2 miles wide. The diversity of its neighborhoods is legendary. Wall Street is located downtown at the southern tip; the garment district, Penn Station, Grand Central Station, and Times Square lay across midtown; and in uptown, Harlem is undergoing revitalization.

New York is known for its open arms to newcomers. Thirty-six percent of the city's population is foreign-born. Immigrants are 43 percent of the New York labor force. They hold a third of the jobs in finance and account for 58 percent of construction workers, half the restaurant and hotel staff, and 40 percent of education, health, and social workers (*The Economist*, 2/19/05). There are many who believe it's immigration that has kept NYC off the road to decline down which other large and old American cities have traveled.

The city has visibly cleaned up its act since the days of out-of-control panhandling, muggings, and burglaries. Indeed, Times Square has been transformed from drug ridden to family friendly, and New York is now rated one of the safest big cities in the United States. That doesn't mean you can leave your wits behind, however. The vast majority of New Yorkers are friendly and will go out of their way to help you if you need it, but there are always a few, well, bad apples.

THE WORKING RICH

New Yorkers are the wealthiest people in the nation. According to the Bureau of Economic Analysis, the per capita personal income for New York City in 2004 was $89,328—markedly higher than the U.S. per capita personal income of $33,050. *The Economist* reports that the residents of 20 streets on the east side of Central Park donated more money to the 2004 presidential campaign than all but five entire American states.

But as a working Joe, don't expect to get rich on your salary. You'll need it to cope with the high cost of living—New York ranks among the most expensive cities in the world, and certainly the highest in the U.S. There are deals to be found if you know where to look (designer knock-off handbags and sunglasses on the street for $5, watches for $20;

60 cents for coffee at the corner cart, or $4 at Starbucks—your choice), but while you can make due with last season's handbag, there's no getting around the biggest expense: housing. In Manhattan, you'll be lucky to find a studio apartment for less than $1,500 or a one-bedroom for $2,000. Prices are a bit lower in Brooklyn, Queens, or Hoboken, New Jersey, and you get more space for the money. Other necessities like food, phone service, and electricity are also more expensive than in other cities. Even flea market fare goes for twice that of other locales.

HELP WANTED...MAYBE

Job growth has been modest and slower than in other parts of the country. While demand is up in many industries (hospitality, health care, and retail), it's losing elsewhere (manufacturing, information, construction). But there is another story that has the economists and city leaders concerned. According to the Fiscal Policy Institute, the average annual pay for the industries increasing job share since 2000 is about $45,000, while the average salary for the industries that have been losing job share is $85,000. The report points out that "while jobs in the expanding sectors like health and educational services are much-needed, economically they are not equivalent to jobs lost in manufacturing, information or finance." Think about it—have you tried to survive in New York on a retail sales salary recently?

Even so, analysts say New York has more than its share of high paying jobs versus the rest of the country. Though the Department of Labor predicts that jobs with the most openings through 2012 are in the low-pay service sector, nurses, accountants, lawyers, first-line supervisors, and wholesale sales reps also rate in the top 25 jobs in demand.

A job hunt in New York is not for the faint of heart. Don't even think of coming here without doing your homework. The best and brightest seek their fortune in New York City, and employers are accustomed to choosing from the cream of the crop. The drop in unemployment mentioned at the beginning of this guide is only part of the story.

Yes, there are more jobs, but there's also more competition. There are many workers who feel steeped in overtime and are nearing burnout, and they've waited for this moment to say "enough is enough." Be prepared to work as hard on your job search as you will once you're employed.

According to the New York State Department of Labor, 3.6 million people hold jobs in New York City. Another 213,600 are unemployed and actively looking for work. To be successful, your job search must be targeted, efficient, and well planned. This Insider Guide is designed to help you compete in the most exciting and competitive job market in the United States: Welcome to New York City.

THE BOTTOM LINE

In New York City, like anywhere, a job search requires patience and persistence. Popular wisdom states that it can take one to two months for every $10,000 you want to make in annual salary to find the right job. The best jobs are found through personal referrals: "We hire people we know," one small NYC business owner told us. You may not personally know the right hiring managers in New York, but someone does. And if you ask enough people, you'll eventually get the leads you need. This is not the time to be shy and self-effacing. New Yorkers are known for their in-your-face attitude. If you're new here, take their example to heart. Be proactive about what you want and where you want to work, and don't be shy about making it known.

Geographic Considerations

While a good many of those who work in the city commute in via Amtrak or other commuter railroads, others who live in Inwood, Washington Heights, Brooklyn, Queens, Hoboken, and Jersey City take the subway into Manhattan. A commute of 45 minutes including a transfer is not unusual.

If you live in Manhattan, perhaps the most prized commute is one that allows you to avoid the subway altogether and walk to work. A 15-minute walk is great, and even a 30-minute walk is considered manageable. Since all the necessities of life are conveniently situated within an average of six blocks of your apartment, walking to work means you can drop off the dry-cleaning and pick up coffee, a bagel, and the *Times* in the morning, and then work out at the gym and pick up wine and flowers on your way home. The restaurant around the corner considers you a regular, and if you don't feel like going out, you can get your meal delivered to your door by the bicycle delivery guys that many restaurants employ.

If you're new to Manhattan, get out and walk. It's the best way to find your way around. Your first purchase should be a street map and a Metrocard. For $2 you can take the subway or local buses. (The Metropolitan Transit Authority system has free subway and bus maps.) A monthly Metrocard is $76. Save your cab fare for the day you have an interview scheduled in the middle of a downpour. (Even then, plan for extra time—traffic will be at a standstill.)

The city is laid out in a grid: The avenues run north and south, and the streets run east and west. It will take you longer to walk a "long block" between the avenues than it will to walk a "short block" north or south. From 59th Street up, Central Park divides Upper Manhattan into the East and West Sides. Because it's difficult to travel from one side to the other, it's not unusual for New Yorkers to live their entire lives—home, work, shopping, dining—on either one side or the other without much crossover.

If you can, structure your commute so that you have only one transfer, either to another subway line or to a bus. Chances are you'll also have to walk at least a few blocks on either end. Also, since it's easier to move north and south on public transportation than it is to travel cross-town, try to arrange for your apartment and place of employment to be located on the same side of the city.

INSIDER TIP

Structure your commute so that you have only one transfer, either to another subway line or to a bus. Chances are you'll also have to walk at least a few blocks on either end. Also, since it's easier to move north and south on public transportation than it is to travel cross-town, try to arrange for your apartment and place of employment to be located on the same side of the city.

Major Industries

Nearly every career and every industry in the United States is represented in the NYC job market. We've summarized the biggest sources of employment in New York City here. Turn to the next chapter for more information about each of these industries and what they have to offer NYC job seekers.

NYC Employment by Sector, May 2006

Sector	Employees
Total nonfarm	**3,657,400**
Total private	**3,100,400**
Educational and health services	702,900
Professional and business services	560,700
Financial activities	451,200
Retail trade	281,600
Information	163,900

Source: New York State Department of Labor.

ADVERTISING

"Americans spend more than anyone else on earth," reports *Advertising Age* (1/10/2006). Indeed the U.S. advertising market is growing (4.5 percent for the first half of 2005) with cable television and Internet outpacing growth in other segments. But in terms of dollar revenue, local newspapers, television, and consumer magazines are the top generators. New York agencies that control most of this revenue are Grey Global Group, McCann Erickson, JWT, and Ogilvy & Mather Worldwide.

ENTERTAINMENT AND SPORTS

Arguably New York City's best-known filmmaker, Woody Allen has done much to promote the dichotomy between New York—known for its vibrant live performing arts scene—and Hollywood—considered the seat of power for film production and television. But thanks to industry consolidation, New York is now home (and thus the source of many jobs) to two of the most powerful broadcast entertainment networks: Fox Entertainment and CBS. The city's creative sector employs 300,000 workers with 11,000 businesses. With the high cost of living threatening New York's position at the top of the creative economy, Mayor Michael Bloomberg has established a public-private partnership to support artists and institutions. The entire NYC metropolitan area boasts 35 radio stations and 100 regional stations, and three Big Five music recording companies are headquartered here. New York City is also home to most of the country's major sports governing bodies and more than its share of sports teams. And consistent with the successful conversion of Times Square from sleaze alley to amusement arcade, Six Flags recently moved its headquarters from the state of Oklahoma to Broadway at 42nd Street.

Nearly every career and every industry in the United States is represented in New York City.

CONSTRUCTION

Walk down any street and you can see (and hear) it. Construction is booming (literally) in New York City. Whether it's the reconstruction of the World Trade Center, the new Moynihan rail station across the street from Penn Station, expansion of the Jacob K. Javits Convention Center, or the various proposed new stadiums, the projects are large-scale, creating a ripple of job opportunities out to far-reaching related fields: supply, shipping, finance, medical services, engineering, architecture, and planning. When completed, the East River Science Park will provide 872,000 square feet of research, retail, and office space for pharmaceutical, medical device production, and biotechnology on 4.5 acres of land next to Bellevue Hospital. The Moynihan Station development will convert the James A. Farley General Post Office into a 300,000-square-foot train station with commercial and residential space—with a $556 million budget for design, development, and construction. In the Bronx, the Food Distribution Center is being developed for food production businesses. Coney Island is embarking on a revitalization of the historic Parachute Pavilion, and Columbia University plans to build a neuroscience research center.

Residential building may be cooling throughout the United States, but not in NYC where new construction permits are up 55 percent from a year ago (1Q 2006). That translates into $665 million in new residential construction for three months alone, an unprecedented figure, according to the city building commissioner as reported on NewYorkBusiness.com.

Major NYC construction employers include Skanska USA, Tishman Construction, Bovis Lend Lease, Structure Tone, and Turner Construction Company, the firm that built Madison Square Garden.

EDUCATION

Teaching in the city's 1,350 public schools can be as difficult as it is fulfilling. Classes are large; resources are low. Only 38 percent of students graduate from high school in four years. The Department of Education comes under city control, rather than state, and there is a ten-year improvement plan in place, starting with training better principals under the NYC Leadership Academy. The city's 80,000 public school teachers have a new contract as of September 2005, with a 15 percent salary increase. Standards for math and English now exist, and 195 new schools are planned. But New York teachers have another option in the thriving private school sector created by parents who begin to jockey for private school placement seemingly from the day their child is born. In fact, one-third of public high school teachers send their own kids to private schools.

The city is the site of several prominent colleges and universities including New York University, the number-one "Dream School" in America (*Princeton Review*, 2004); Columbia University, which includes Barnard College; and the left-leaning New School.

FASHION

Given New York's historic garment district, it's natural that the city should be home base to America's most prominent apparel designers and manufacturers: Ann Taylor, Tommy Hilfiger, Polo Ralph Lauren, and Liz Claiborne. Seventh Avenue is the center runway for the area bounded by 6th and 9th Avenues; the Fashion Institute of Technology, the world's largest fashion design school, is at 27th Street. Walk around the block from FIT and you'll be in the fur district (Yikes! Are those mink heads dangling in the window?), and a few blocks toward 6th Avenue is the millinery section. Your employment search might take you outside this box to SoHo for instance, or further east to 28th and Madison Avenue where the intimate apparel showrooms are clustered. There's a burgeoning showcase for emerging designers in lower Manhattan with MetroNY and EdgeNY, where young fashion and jewelry entrepreneurs sell directly to the public. In addition to FIT, New York hosts the Parsons School of Design and the Laboratory Institute of Merchandising.

FINANCE AND INSURANCE

Wall Street is the physical site of the New York Stock Exchange and the figurative vortex for the world's financial marketplace. Twenty of the top 25 foreign branches of international banks are represented in New York, plus eight of the top ten securities firms, 219 international banks, and five of the country's ten largest insurance companies. We're talking commercial banks, savings banks, credit card businesses, trust companies, insurance companies (life, casualty, property, and health), investment banks, and asset managers. The largest players include Citigroup, JPMorgan Chase, Goldman Sachs, Bank of New York, Merrill Lynch, American Express, MetLife, and the Prudential headquarters in Newark, New Jersey.

HEALTH CARE

Health care is by far the largest sector with the most job opportunities in New York City, with 16 percent of employers and 1.1 million jobs. After all, it takes a lot of professionals to care for 8 million people. New York and the surrounding region are home to 25 medical research institutions, 70 hospitals, and 40,000 doctors; the National Institute of Health funds $1.3 billion in research and much of that goes to NYC hospitals creating lots of well-funded medical research jobs. Hospitals are major employers: New York–Presbyterian Healthcare System; Continuum Health Partners, which operates Beth Israel Medical Center, St. Luke's–Roosevelt Hospital Center, Long Island College Hospital, and the New York Eye and Ear Infirmary; Saint Vincent Catholic Medical Centers; Mount Sinai Medical Center; and the Memorial Sloan-Kettering Cancer Center. New York HMOs with the most primary care physicians are UnitedHealthcare, Cigna HealthCare of New York, WellChoice (a.k.a. Empire Blue Cross and Blue Shield), and Oxford Health Plans. WellChoice, UnitedHealthcare, and Cigna are also among the top ten largest PPOs in New York.

HOSPITALITY AND FOOD SERVICE

Restaurants are responsible for the largest market share of the hospitality and food service industry segment, followed by hotels. Cafes comprise the smallest. Waitpeople can choose from 2,630 annual job openings in New York, with another 2,540 for pastry chefs and cooks. Large New York employers include Hilton New York, which also owns the famed Waldorf Astoria; Sheraton New York Hotel & Towers; and the world's leading hotel chain, represented by the New York Marriott Marquis, though Marriott is not headquartered here. The renowned Plaza Hotel is closed for remodeling, but there are several new high-profile hotel projects on board, including a conversion of the former MetLife headquarters at One Madison Avenue by hotelier Ian Schrager. JetBlue Airways is headquartered here, and online grocer, FreshDirect, is also a New Yorker.

LAW

INSIDER TIP

Health care is by far the largest sector with the most job opportunities in New York City.

The legal service industry is the second-largest professional service industry in the nation, second only to health services. Manhattan law firms are the most profitable per partner in the country. Three of the ten top-ranked firms based on gross revenue are located here: Skadden, Arps, Slate, Meagher & Flom; White & Case; and Weil, Gotshal & Manges. Twenty-two Manhattan law firms earned more than $1 million per partner.

MANAGEMENT CONSULTING

Management consulting is an $80 billion enterprise within the United States and a $100 billion industry worldwide. Specialties include general strategy, information technology, marketing and branding, leadership, logistics, human resources, and industry-specific practices. Given the number of companies based in New York, it's no wonder that the metropolitan area is home to five of the world's ten largest consulting firms: McKinsey & Company, IBM Global Services, Accenture, Deloitte Consulting, and Mercer.

MANUFACTURING (INCLUDES CONSUMER PRODUCTS AND PHARMACEUTICALS)

Once the largest manufacturing center in the country with one million jobs, New York now has half that and continued to lose jobs in the past year. The state of New York ranks fourth in terms of the number of manufacturing establishments in operation. In the city, the sector is primarily clothing and printing. Amerada Hess Corp. and Colgate-Palmolive are headquartered here as is defense contractor L-3 Communications. However, there is much good news in the vibrant sector of pharmaceuticals and biotechnology. New York is home to 90 bioscience companies, two biotech incubators, and pharmaceutical giants Pfizer and Bristol-Myers Squibb. Thirty new biotech companies are launched here every year.

PUBLISHING

Publishing in the United States is a $100 billion industry, and New York City is its capital. This is where the romance of the publishing industry becomes reality. It's the business that inspired the Katharine Hepburn–Spencer Tracy movie mystique, and it is the site of the renowned *New York Times* and the famed *New Yorker* magazine. Advertising accounts for more than half the industry's revenue, and book sales generate about a quarter. Newspapers employ the most people; magazines the least. The most visible employment opportunities are in editorial (reporting, writing, and editing), design, and photography; many of these folks become celebrities on par with those they cover (think of the late fashion photographer Richard Avedon or Helen Gurley Brown of *Cosmopolitan*), but there are legions of workers involved in the less glamorous but just as important work of production, circulation, advertising sales, promotion, accounting, warehousing, and distribution.

Major players include Time Warner; Random House; Harper Collins; Penguin; Simon & Schuster; McGraw-Hill (*Business Week*); Hearst (*Cosmopolitan* and *Esquire* magazines); the New York mayor's company, financial information distributor Bloomberg; and Scholastic, the publisher of the *Harry Potter* series. Magazine publisher Advance Publications (*Vogue* and *Allure*) is located on Staten Island and also owns 25 daily U.S. newspapers.

REAL ESTATE

Manhattan's meteoric property values have attracted a goodly share of fortune-seekers to the real estate industry—along with stories of poor timing. How many versions of "My uncle sold his condo for $198,000 in 1991 and now it's worth $1.2 million," have you heard? There are six real estate investment trusts on *Crain's* 2006 list of the top 50 fastest growing New York firms.

For many, brokering real estate has become the new waitperson/bartending job. Actors and other artists have discovered that the flexible hours in real estate make it a suitable way to earn additional income while auditioning for their next big role. Major segments of this industry include developers, property managers, and real estate agents and brokers. The real estate sector takes an active interest in supporting a healthy sales environment. It sponsors New York Safe & Secure, a training program for security officers in commercial office buildings.

Major NYC players include industry giant Cendant Corp.; The Trump Organization; and The Lefrak Organization, which owns the Battery Park City development. Silverstein Properties controls the redevelopment of the World Trade Center site; but it's a California firm, Alexandria Real Estate Equities, that will develop the East River Science Park on the Bellevue Hospital campus.

RETAIL

Manhattan has been described by some as a giant mall, but the only true mega-mall is the new Time Warner Center at Columbus Center, which houses a gigantic Whole Foods. Retail salespersons and cashiers top the list of job openings in New York as projected through 2012. While you'll see nearly every retail chain in the nation represented on New York streets, you won't find Wal-Mart among them. The New York City Council has successfully kept the discount chain outside the city's borders because of its benefits and employment policies. Licensed street vendors are everywhere, either attracting shoppers to or competing with shop owners, depending on your point of view. The sale of nondurable goods (for example, food and clothing) accounts for the majority of the local retail industry.

The third-largest department store chain, Federated Department Stores (Macy's and Bloomingdale's) is the leading retail employer in New York. The city also serves as headquarters for Toys R Us and Barnes & Noble. The Great Atlantic & Pacific Tea Company chain of grocery stores is headquartered in Montvale, New Jersey.

TECHNOLOGY

Technology is a $9.2 billion industry in New York City, with some 4,000 high-tech and new media companies. Digital media has exploded—HDTV, DVDs, IPTV, cell phone video, iPod video, podcasting, videopodcasting. The New York Software Industry Association has referred to the digital media business environment in Manhattan as the "wild, wild West," with standards and strategies still at the pioneering stages. One newcomer is Orchestria with active policy management software that stops spamming and hacking before the email delivery or the illegal transaction is completed. The industry represents an important source of employment to not only highly skilled software developers and project managers, but to accounting, marketing, and human resources professionals as well.

INSIDER TIP

Technology is a $9.2-billion industry in New York City, with some 4,000 high-tech and new media companies.

The local industry consists primarily of small to midsize companies. Some of the more recognizable local names include IBM and Atari. Microsoft, based in Seattle, is adding 140 jobs to double its Manhattan staff because its 400 largest corporate clients are located here.

TELECOMMUNICATIONS

Like other large cities, New York City is working on getting its own telecommunications house in order. That the metropolitan area is host to some of the major league players in the industry should help: Verizon Communications, Lucent, Cablevision Systems Corp., NTL, Lexent, Verint, and Avaya. In 2005, the mayor announced a public-private partnership to improve and expand capacity for wireless technology, encourage development of new technology, and educate small business owners on how broadband can help them run their businesses. The telecommunications market in New

York City includes local, long distance, and international telephone services as well as cellular and paging services, and Internet access through broadband and wireless technology. The city hosts a robust equipment manufacturing sector, focusing on modems and networking equipment for mature markets, such as that in the United States, and providing the basics (phones, answering machines, and switching equipment) to developing markets.

New York City Employers, by Industry (2005)

Industry	Firms	Total Employees	Percent of Total (%)
Private sector	220,099	2,945,839	100
Utilities	49	14,703	0.5
Construction	11,126	109,750	3.7
Manufacturing	7,184	113,155	3.8
Wholesale trade	16,004	137,247	4.7
Retail trade	27,977	275,876	9.4
Transportation and warehousing	4,297	99,188	3.4
Information	5,238	150,855	5.1
Finance and insurance	10,718	320,654	10.9
Real estate rental and leasing	19,528	115,548	3.9
Professional tech and scientific	23,568	292,375	9.9
Management of companies	1,016	55,453	1.9
Admin., support, and waste services	7,722	184,544	6.3
Education services	2,707	123,874	4.2
Health care and social assistance	18,335	524,901	17.8
Arts, entertainment, and recreation	4,259	59,965	2.0
Accommodation and food services	14,355	210,863	7.2
Other services excl. public admin.	27,640	134,940	4.6
Unclassified and other	18,321	21,708	0.7

Source: New York State Department of Labor

Employment Trends and Outlook

EMPLOYMENT TRENDS

Unemployment is down, job growth is up. But don't call it a buyer's market yet. For one thing, the nagging concern over energy costs and questions about sustainability mean employers continue to make conservative choices.

Since March 2005, New York City has added 58,200 jobs, a 1.6 percent increase, which is consistent with the rest of the nation. Hiring is particularly hot in leisure and hospitality, education and health services, and financial activities, where jobs grew 4 percent, 2.6 percent, and 2 percent respectively during 2005. And thanks to the Sarbanes-Oxley Act, entry-level accountants are in demand. Employment data for New York City reflects a trend toward a service-based, rather than a manufacturing-based, economy. At least 73 percent of total employment is within service-oriented industries.

While job hunters report long searches and stiff competition, unemployment in New York City is lower than it's been since the dotcom crash in 2000. At 5.5 percent for March 2006, the city's unemployment remains higher than the national average of 4.7 percent but well below the 8 percent rates of 2002 and the whopping high of 9.1 percent in January 2003.

The city's economy is on a continuing upswing, but has not completely recovered from the effects of 9/11. As of September 2005, total job count is 3.9 percent less than the September 2,000 peak. NYC economic growth is consistent with the rest of the nation, but if it seems to you the cost of living is rising faster, you're right. Inflation in NYC is 3.9 percent versus 3.4 percent elsewhere. The New York gross city product was up 3.4 percent for 2005 versus 3.5 percent for the nation.

If you haven't conducted a job search recently, be prepared for some changes. "You have to have a lot of patience," advises one NYC job seeker. "Even though the market has opened up, it's [still] much in the favor of the employer. It can be tough. They can be nitpicky and take their time with the process." The years of layoffs, tight budgets, and work redistribution has changed the employment marketplace in other key ways:

Greater Specificity

You're likely to encounter hiring managers who want exact matches of skills and experience to their job requisitions. "In financial services, it's not enough to know about finance. You have to know derivatives or mortgages," says a job seeker. "There are jobs out there, but they want you to have very specific experience," says an art director. There are so many candidates that employers can afford to be choosy.

Risk Aversion

After the painful lessons learned while trimming the payroll fat over the past three years, hiring managers are playing it safe. Many companies are continuing to outsource in lieu of increasing headcount and its attendant overhead. And when organizations do

Employment data for New York City reflects a trend toward a service-based, rather than a manufacturing-based, economy. At least 73 percent of total employment is within service-oriented industries.

Persistence, persuasion, and patience are your best tools for the job hunt; job growth is moderate overall, and the competition is intense. Employers are willing to hold out for a near-perfect match to their job. Most won't take the time to puzzle out whether or not you qualify. It's up to you to make it crystal clear.

add staff, they tend to stick with people they know. Rather than placing job requisitions with search firms or posting openings on job boards, they might recruit known talent from competitors or offer temporary or part-time positions. The story of one small New York–based financial services firm isn't unusual: A partner waited the duration of his noncompete agreement before raiding the ranks of his former employer for the specific person he wanted to hire. "We called up the day after [the noncompete agreement expired] and two weeks later the guy was on our payroll."

EMPLOYMENT OUTLOOK

In New York City, certain jobs are expected to be in greater demand over the next five to six years. Opportunities will be strong for those in sales, health care, and education, for example, with fewer hires in the sciences, architecture, engineering, and legal professions.

The nationwide trend toward more contract or hourly hires (usually without benefits) and fewer full-time hires is also likely to be reflected in New York City, perhaps to a greater degree than that seen nationally, as the pool of available skilled workers is so great.

New York City's Top Industries, by Total Employment

Rank	Industry	Total NYC Employment	Average Annual NYC Openings
1	Sales and related	400,720	12,990
2	Health care	383,670	12,840
3	Education, training, and library	266,520	11,520
4	Business and financial operations	201,870	5,120
5	Arts, design, entertainment, sports, and media	139,410	4,480
6	Computer and mathematical	94,450	4,030
7	Legal	67,020	1,430
8	Community and social services	64,080	2,480
9	Architecture and engineering	40,200	1,070
10	Life, physical, and social science	27,920	1,120

Source: New York State Department of Labor: Projected Growth in New York City Jobs, 2000–2010

New York City's 25 Fastest-Growing Occupations

Rank	Occupation	Industry or Career
1	Medical assistants	Health care
2	Physician assistants	Health care
3	Physical therapist assistants	Health care
4	Network systems and data communications analysts	Information technology
5	Physical therapist aides	Health care
6	Amusement and recreation attendants	Hospitality
7	Computer software engineers, systems software	Information technology
8	Fitness trainers and aerobics instructors	Personal care
9	Occupational therapist assistants	Health care
10	Personal financial advisers	Finance
11	Athletic trainers	Personal care
12	Hazardous materials removal workers	Construction
13	Medical records and health information technicians	Health care
14	Respiratory therapy technicians	Health care
15	Dental assistants	Health care
16	Mental health and substance abuse social workers	Social services
17	Database administrators	Information technology
18	Personal and home-care aides	Health care
19	Cardiovascular technologists and technicians	Health care
20	Veterinary technologists and technicians	Health care
21	Physical therapists	Health care
22	Respiratory therapists	Health care
23	Computer systems analysts	Information technology
24	Computer software engineers, applications	Information technology
25	Social and human services assistants	Social services

Source: New York State Department of Labor: Projected Growth in New York City Jobs, 2002–2012; industry/field information added by WetFeet

Where the Jobs Are

Getting Your Bearings

Major Industries

Major Careers

Employer Rankings

Getting Your Bearings

Assessing the array of job opportunities in a city the size of New York is no easy task. To help you get the lay of the land, we profile the city's largest and most promising industries and careers in this chapter. But before you jump in, you'll need to know not only what's in yonder wood but also how to find what you (in your infinite uniqueness) really need without retracing your steps needlessly.

HOW WE ARRIVED HERE

Bear with us for a moment, as we explain what may at first appear to be arbitrary distinctions.

In this chapter, *career* has a very specific definition: It refers to any functional occupation that spans unrelated industries, such as accounting, human resources, and marketing. The careers profiled in the "Major Careers" section are those that are more or less consistent across industries and thus tend to allow greater cross-industry job mobility for those employed in these ubiquitous fields. For example, a human resources (HR) manager with insurance industry experience need not limit his job search to opportunities with other insurance companies. He is just as likely to land an equivalent or better HR position in an altogether different industry. Why? Because his skill set and professional experience are assumed to be on a par with that of HR managers in other industries. Industry-specific knowledge and experience are not as valued in these professions as they are in others. Naturally, there are exceptions, but our insiders concur that this is generally the case.

It's worth noting that there are many careers other than those profiled in the "Major Careers" section, but few are as industry-independent. For example, "Analyst" and "Customer Service Representative" are job titles common to many industries, but the work for each varies considerably depending on the industry. For any occupation that relies heavily on industry-specific expertise, the candidate's job search is better limited to the industry in question (and perhaps related industries).

What does all this mean to you? As you review the information in this chapter and use it to target your own job search, you will need to answer the question: "Is the kind of work I hope to find specific to a few industries, or does it span many disparate ones?"

FROM POINT A TO B: HOW TO USE THIS CHAPTER

In this section, we describe the three common types of job seekers: (1) those with no idea where they're headed ("Not a Clue What You Want to Do"), (2) those with some idea ("Know Where You Want to Go, But Not Sure How to Get There"), and (3) those with very specific ideas ("So, You've Always Wanted to Be a …?"). To get the most out of this chapter, select the job-seeker description that best matches your own feelings and follow the recommendations in that section.

Not a Clue What You Want to Do?

If you aren't sure what you want to do, don't panic! Take a little time to enjoy the freedom of so many options. We recommend that you read all of the profiles in this chapter and think seriously about which sound like a good match for your interests, strengths, education, and experience. As you think about which industries and careers might interest you, remember that it's important to keep your focus neither too narrow nor too broad. In other words, don't feel you must narrow your selection to a single career or industry, but do force yourself to eliminate some options.

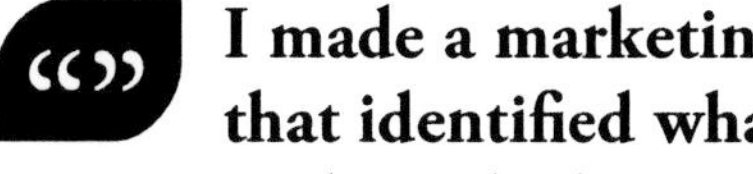

I made a marketing plan that identified what I want to do and where I want to do it. I identified 50 companies that I think are places where I might want to work.

And don't let yourself be paralyzed by indecision: To ensure that your current vocational confusion doesn't derail your job search before it starts, you should select at least two or three potential paths initially, so you can move forward and become accustomed to the process.

Don't worry! Your decisions aren't final, and you are welcome—nay, encouraged—to reconsider your path should you find that it isn't what you hoped for.

Know Where You Want to Go, But Not Sure How to Get There?

If you have a general idea of the kind of work you'd like to pursue and have the appropriate educational background, some relevant experience, or both, your task is a little easier. You probably fit one of these two descriptions:

You have a specific industry (or two) in mind but are unsure of the role you'd like to play within that industry. If this sounds like you, we recommend that you review the industry profiles that match your interest first and then read the entire "Major Careers" section. While reading the industry and career profiles, think about which roles are consistent with your strengths, education, and experience. You may need to do some additional research online to learn about the positions that interest you. WetFeet provides dozens of career and industry profiles online (www.wetfeet.com), which are not specific to New York City, but include job descriptions and much more that doesn't appear in this book. You can also read WetFeet's Real People Profiles online to learn how real people working in these fields describe what they do. Your goal is to identify several potential positions you want to target in your job search. Then you can use the relevant list of major industry players to get thinking about the companies you want to consider.

You are drawn to a specific career but unsure of which industries you should target. If this describes you, we recommend that you start out by flipping to the "Major Careers" section first and determining whether your desired career is profiled there.

If it is, read that profile and then flip back to the "Major Industries" section. Read through the industry profiles and focus on those that interest you. You can target your job search across several industries if appropriate. To learn even more, do your own research online. And don't forget to check out the additional resources included at the end of each profile in this chapter.

Don't despair if your career of choice is not profiled in the "Major Careers" section. That just means that you're likely to be limited to a smaller set of potential industries. You will need to read the "Major Industries" profiles to find out which industries are appropriate targets for your job search. Keep in mind that these profiles are not exhaustive: If your career isn't mentioned in an industry profile that otherwise interests you, use your own judgment and understanding of the career to consider whether it's likely to be a role prevalent in that industry.

If you're still not sure, you can easily check the "Careers" section of the largest industry players' websites to see whether they fill positions that are comparable to your hoped-for career. You can do additional research on WetFeet.com to learn even more about the industries that interest you.

So, You've Always Wanted to Be a...?

If, for example, you have your heart set on a career in the fashion industry, by all means, go directly to that profile. After you've finished reading, spend some time in the "Major Careers" section, because most of those profiles will also be relevant to fashion. Think about specific types of positions you'll look for, and then target the major players.

Perhaps your clarity of purpose, professionally speaking, is the result of hard-earned experience. You have worked in your target career, industry, or both for at least a few years and you bought this book already armed with a clear idea of the kind of work that you'll be pursuing. If this describes you, go ahead and skip to the industry and career profiles that are relevant to your job search. There you'll find specific information about what distinguishes this industry in New York City, including average salaries and leading NYC companies.

Major Industries

The 16 NYC industries profiled here dominate the city's employment landscape: They are the top hirers and employers, and they generate the most interest among job seekers.

These profiles are not intended to provide in-depth information about the nationwide state of these industries or other detailed information that is not unique or specific to the NYC market. That information is readily available elsewhere.

Instead, we have included general industry information only as it relates to hiring and recent trends, or where otherwise needed for context. Each industry profile describes the current state of the industry in New York City, relevant national trends, job prospects for the near future, average NYC salaries for key jobs, a list of top industry players that have their U.S. headquarters in New York City or have a presence in the city that represents a significant portion of the company's total U.S. business. Each profile concludes with a list of additional resources that readers are encouraged to consult.

The following industries are profiled in this section:

- Advertising
- Construction
- Education (and educational services)
- Entertainment and Sports (includes television and film production, and performing arts)
- Fashion
- Finance and Insurance (includes banking, investment banking, retail brokerage, and banking-related services)
- Health Care

- Hospitality and Food Service
- Law
- Management Consulting
- Manufacturing (includes consumer products, industrial, and pharmaceutical manufacturers)
- Publishing
- Real Estate
- Retail Trade
- Technology (high-tech and new media)
- Telecommunications

ADVERTISING

Legendary Madison Avenue is more of a concept than an actual physical address for advertising agencies these days. But New York City is still headquarters to such heavy hitters as JWT (formerly J. Walter Thompson), McCann Erickson, BBDO Worldwide, DDB Worldwide, and Grey Global Group. The automobile industry is the largest U.S. advertiser, followed by food, financial services, cosmetics/toiletries, drugs, beverages/snacks, and restaurants. Don't rule out the smaller firms in your job search: The top five advertising companies represent only 27.4 percent of the market.

Like so many other industries, advertising firms have experienced a lot of consolidation in recent years, as companies join forces to lower costs and stay competitive in the global marketplace. In advertising, bigger size means more clout with media outlets and, therefore, lower advertising costs. Plus, by owning multiple advertising agencies, a single holding company can control several competing accounts without presenting conflict of interest, whereas a single agency cannot hold accounts with competing companies.

Hiring note: Account planning—also known as *strategic planning*—was developed in English ad agencies in the 1960s and 1970s. It took a while, but in recent years the American advertising industry has discovered account planning in a big way. Account planning is a discipline that aims to increase understanding of the consumer. Today, account planning is such an integral part of many American ad agencies that it's the account planners who do most of the strategizing on behalf of clients, rather than the account management staff.

Job Prospects

Though boutique agencies are growing in number and revenue, the big names continue to handle most of the accounts—and earn most of the dollars. They also are the primary source of employment opportunities. In addition to the size of the firm, you'll need to think about its location, its client list, and the kind of advertising it does: branding vs. promotional, general vs. specific industries, general vs. specific media.

Advertising is a difficult industry to get a start in, so there is a whole lot of competition for relatively few low-paying jobs. Be prepared to begin at the bottom and work your contacts to move to higher levels.

Although some of the bigger agencies do recruit on campus for entry-level account management positions, most entry-level hires are not recruited. The easiest routes into the marketing and business side of advertising are entry-level media jobs and administrative assistant jobs. They don't pay very well, and they involve lots of grunt work, but you'll get a chance to show your stuff and get promoted. If you're a creative, you can't get a job in advertising without a book of your work. For entry-level copywriting or art-direction positions, this means designing and producing mock advertisements.

Key Advertising Jobs

Key Job	Median NYC Salary ($)	Average Entry-Level NYC Salary ($)
Account executive	123,640	70,760
Copywriter	50,020	27,290
Graphic designer	53,490	32,100
Art director	90,790	54,570
Public relations specialist	50,360	32,990

Sources: New York State Department of Labor; WetFeet research

Resources

AAAAgencySearch.com (www.aaaagencysearch.com)

Advertising Age (www.adage.com)

The Advertising Club of New York (www.theadvertisingclub.org)

Advertising Research Foundation (www.arfsite.org)

AdWeek (www.adweek.com)

American Association of Advertising Agencies (www.aaaa.org)

Association of National Advertisers (www.ana.net/hr/hr.htm)

Careers in Advertising & Public Relations
(WetFeet Insider Guide, available from www.wetfeet.com)

New York Times Media & Advertising section
(www.nytimes.com/pages/business/media)

Key NYC Advertising Firms

Firm	2005 Revenue ($M)	1-Yr. Change (%)	Employees	Website
Omnicom Group	10,481	7.5	61,000	www.omnicomgroup.com
Interpublic Group of Companies	6,274	–1.8	43,000	www.interpublic.com
Euro RSCG Worldwide*	1,350	n/a	11,000	www.eurorscg.com
BBDO Worldwide*	1,326	7.2	17,200	www.bbdo.com
JWT Company	1,325	12.5	9,000	www.jwt.com
Grey Global Group**	1,307	9.0	10,500	www.greyglobalgroup.com
McCann Worldgroup**	1,220	3.7	n/a	www.mccann.com
Horizon Media	1,200	n/a	325	www.horizonmedia.com
Young & Rubicam Brands*	1,180	5.4	12,700	www.yrbrands.com
DDB Worldwide Communications Group*	1,023	8.4	8,833	www.ddb.com
Monster Worldwide	987	16.7	5,000	www.monsterworldwide.com
TBWA Worldwide*	838	8.7	8,700	www.tbwa.com
Ogilvy & Mather Worldwide*	753	6.6	12,000	www.ogilvy.com
Saatchi & Saatchi Worldwide**	543	14.0	7,000	www.saatchi.com
Foote Cone & Belding Worldwide*	499	10.4	n/a	www.fcb.com
Deutsch, Inc*	345	10.6	1,036	www.deutschinc.com
Arbitron	310	4.5	1,345	www.arbitron.com
Corinthian Media	310	n/a	67	www.mediabuying.com
DoubleClick	302	11.2	1,541	www.doubleclick.com
Publicis USA*	280	11.5	800	www.publicis-usa.com

*2004 figures
**2003 figures
Sources: *Advertising Age*; American Association of Advertising Agencies; *Crain's New York Business Book of Lists 2006*; Hoover's; WetFeet analysis

CONSTRUCTION

New York construction is up. Not only are residential building permits at unprecedented high levels, but some of the most prestigious commercial building projects in the world are either underway or on the boards in New York. Most famous of course is the redevelopment of the World Trade Center (WTC) under control of Silverstein Properties. Heavyweight architects Lord Richard Rogers of Britain and Fumihiko Maki of Japan will design two of the WTC buildings and are involved in other prestigious projects such as the expansion of the United Nations Building, the East River waterfront, and the Javits Convention Center. So you can bet there will be plenty of work for all New York–based architectural firms, not to mention civil engineering and construction companies.

The residential market here differs from that of other cities in that there are virtually no single-family, freestanding houses. Residences come in the form of high rises. It's hard to imagine how NYC could get any more crowded, but the New York City building commissioner told NewYorkBusiness.com in April that many areas of the city allow for even greater housing density than currently exists. There is also a healthy remodeling subsector of the industry that provides business for the city's electricians, carpenters, painters, interior designers, and feng shui consultants.

Job Prospects

The majority of jobs are for union-card-carrying tradespeople and laborers, but there are also supporting staff jobs that aren't unionized. "There is an incredible amount of work right now, and it spills over into all the related fields," reports a construction management insider. The trick is how to learn about what openings are where. It's unlikely you'll find construction industry jobs at a job fair or listed online. "You have to find where and who the companies are, and you have to walk in," he says. "We have people walk up to the construction site and ask who they can talk to in the company. You have to find names. You have to be very personal. It's an old-school network."

"Construction is hungry for people," says the same insider. "It's not just engineering firms, it's suppliers, designers, shippers, record keepers, medical people, planners, air conditioning and heating specialists, accountants. It takes all these people." The jobs are specialized and many require licensing. Opportunities for professionals exist in engineering, design, and safety inspection. Among professional hires, demand for civil engineers is greater than for most other positions.

Key Construction Jobs

Key Job	Median NYC Salary ($)	Average Entry-Level NYC Salary ($)
Architect	64,190	41,910
Civil engineer	73,710	53,070
Construction manager	99,190	64,600
Drafter	46,110	32,420
Electrical engineer	84,740	57,510
Safety officer	61,450	42,940
Building inspector	52,300	36,500
Equipment operator engineer	78,940	55,110
Painter	50,480	25,850

Sources: New York State Department of Labor; WetFeet research

Resources

AEC WorkForce (www.aecworkforce.com)

Home Builders Institute (www.hbi.org)

McGraw-Hill Construction (www.construction.com)

National Society of Professional Engineers (www.nspe.org)

Society of Women Engineers (www.swe.org)

Key NYC Construction Companies

Company	2005 Revenue ($M)	NYC Employees	Website
Turner Construction Company	2,125	1050	www.turnerconstruction.com
Skanska USA	1,810	562	www.skanskausa.com
Parsons Brinckerhoff, Inc.	1,450	n/a	www.pbworld.com
Tishman Construction Corp.	1,310	505	www.tishmanconstruction.com
The Structure Tone Organization	1,258	593	www.structuretone.com
Bovis Lend Lease LMB	1,128	610	www.bovislendlease.com
Berger Group Holdings	707	4,578	www.louisberger.com
Plaza Construction Group	508	256	www.plazaconstruction.com
Torcon Inc.	398	205	www.torcon.com
HRH Construction	396	181	www.hrhconstruction.com
Hebegan Construction	350	75	www.hennegan.com
Kreisler Borg Florman	340	106	www.kbfgeneral.com
Gotham Construction Co.	249	75	www.gothamconstruction.com
M.A. Angellades, Inc.	165	155	www.ma-angeliades.com
Perini Corp.	164	87	www.perini.com
VRH Construction Corp.	160	88	www.vrhcorp.com
TDX Construction	144	147	www.tdxconstruction.com
Worth Construction	120	52	www.worthconstruction.com
Americon Inc.	102	66	www.americoninc.com
Andron	100	50	www.androncc.com
Ibex Consruction	90	80	www.ibexconsruction.com

Source: *Crain's New York Book of Lists 2006*

EDUCATION

While schools around the nation are closing their doors, New York City has a plan to open 195 new ones. Public schools in New York City fall under the jurisdiction of the city rather than the state. The system is working to reduce crime in some of the city's most problem-ridden schools, train principals to be more effective, and hire 100 new teachers by June 2006. Most wanted are math, science, and special-ed teachers for the toughest schools. As an incentive, the Department of Education now provides a housing subsidy.

Though the biggest education employers in New York City are universities, there are also many opportunities in corporate training, vocational education, and library services. Special education teachers and preschool and childcare administrators are among the fastest-growing occupational groups in the city. New York also has one of the largest sectors of private primary and secondary schools in the United States. On the whole, private school teachers earn less than their public school counterparts, and though school management competence varies (look into the director's fundraising track record as well as educational philosophy), the environment of private schools is often more supportive of teachers' needs.

Opportunities are also available in education-oriented businesses, which teach subjects that fall outside the scope of traditional schools. Thus, there are companies such as the Kaplan-owned SCORE! Educational Centers, which help kids improve grades, as well as Kaplan proper (owned by the Washington Post Company) and the Princeton Review to prepare students for the SAT, GMAT, and other exams. Brain Pop is a new media company that publishes educational materials. SchoolNet, Inc., with its Web-based instructional management software for K–12 school districts, has $3.3 million in annual sales and closed a $3-million financing deal in 2006. Foreign-language schools also fit into the education sector, as do a plethora of business, computer, and self-help companies. Test-prep and tutoring operations, in particular, are looking extremely healthy these days. SparkNotes, the youngest cousin of classic study aid CliffsNotes, for example, is owned by New York–based Barnes & Noble.

Special Note for Women: New York University is among the five best employers for women in New York City (New York Commission on Women's Issues).

Job Prospects

Overall, according to the Bureau of Labor Statistics (BLS), the number of people employed in elementary and secondary education is expected to grow at the same rate as the average for all other occupations—but because many teachers are reaching retirement age, aspiring teachers will have excellent job prospects. At the postsecondary level, teachers can expect more opportunities in coming years, as the kids of baby boomers graduate from high school and increase college and university enrollment. Distance-learning opportunities are also expected to grow.

Higher education provides a host of opportunities in positions rarely found in the K–12 segment: investment manager, alumni fundraiser, financial-aid officer, admissions officer, buildings and grounds manager, and the like.

In most cases, if you want to teach K–12, you'll have to get certification, and for college-level positions at least a master's is necessary. If you don't have the credentials, though, don't despair. You might still be able to land a job in an under-resourced (that is, under-funded, inner-city) school district. In New York, check out the NYC Teaching Fellows program that pays people to teach while they're getting their credentials. You can also work at a private school; many hire recent grads. Be prepared to earn meager wages, though. Suburban public schools generally offer the best K–12 salaries.

Lots of recent college grads find positions at education-oriented businesses to get a taste of teaching before moving on to more traditional schools. Others go on to make a career out of educational services work. Such organizations prefer experienced hires, but many will train new employees or expect them to learn on the job. Positions with these organizations can offer opportunities for international travel and business experience. Downsides for job seekers include low pay, little job security, and few chances for advancement.

Finally, those working in special education or in English as a second language (ESL) are expected to enjoy growing job opportunities in coming years.

Key Education Jobs

Key Job	Median NYC Salary ($)	Average Entry-Level NYC Salary($)
University professor	51,570–103,020	28,990–76,740
Elementary school teacher	77,680	51,270
Corporate training manager	97,980	58,720
High school teacher	85,590	61,650
Nursing instructor	77,580	49,080
Preschool teacher	36,580	24,840
Principal	97,520	80,810
Vocational ed teacher	43,860	25,050
Librarian	49,490	37,930
School counselor	55,680	35,500

Sources: New York State Department of Labor; WetFeet research

Resources

Education Week (www.edweek.org)

National Education Association (www.nea.org)

New York City Department of Education (www.nycenet.edu)

New York State Department of Education (www.nysed.gov)

Key NYC Educational Organizations

Organization	2005 Revenue ($M)	1-Yr. Change (%)	Employees	Website
Columbia University	2,501	13.7	12,631	www.columbia.edu
New York University**	2,005	7.5	15,010	www.nyu.edu
City University of New York*	1,371	15	33,460	www.cuny.edu
Kaplan*	1,135	35.4	7,600	www.kaplan.com
Yeshiva University**	447	n/a	n/a	www.yu.edu
Edison Schools**	425	–8.5	n/a	www.edisonschools.com
Fordham University**	306	17.8	n/a	www.fordham.edu
St. John's University*	315	6.5	2,803	www.stjohns.edu
Long Island University**	312	10.4	n/a	www.liu.edu
Pace University**	224	7.6	n/a	www.pace.edu
The New School	187	n/a	3,533	www.newschool.edu
The Princeton Review	131	14.7	470	www.princetonreview.com
American Management Assn.**	129	–22.6	700	www.amanet.org
Katharine Gibbs	76.0	n/a	400	www.gibbsny.edu
School of Visual Arts	68.2	n/a	1,400	www.schoolofvisualarts.edu
Fashion Institute of Technology	67.1	n/a	1212	www.fitnyc.edu
The Juilliard School**	51.4	n/a	n/a	www.juilliard.edu

*2004 figures
**2003 figures
Sources: Hoover's; WetFeet analysis

ENTERTAINMENT AND SPORTS

From Broadway to baseball, New York has more than its share of stars. Its symphony, opera, and ballet companies are world-class. The Metropolitan Museum of Art and the Guggenheim rank right along with their European cousins. Carnegie Hall in midtown hosts the best musicians of the world, and down the street, Radio City Music Hall boasts the synchronized kick line of the Rockettes. Walk by the Rockefeller Center any weekday morning and catch the crowd checking out Matt Lauer and Meredith Vieira (Katie Couric's replacement) on the *Today Show*. Chances are that your personal trainer at the gym is a former Broadway chorus dancer, and your real estate rental agent may reschedule a showing so he can catch an audition.

This is a glamorous industry, but aside from the athletes with the Yankees or prima ballerinas with the New York City Ballet, it's a largely underemployed, underpaid population. In a 2006 report by the Freelancer's Union, 40 percent of the city's creative workers made less than $35,000 in 2005. Many have no health insurance and avoid seeking medical care.

Film and television production in New York City has grown over the past five years and the city now competes on a level financial playing field with Los Angeles. With 145 studios and 740,000 square feet of production space, one-third of all independent films are produced in New York City. Of the 35 radio stations in the city, Arbitron (a NYC-based provider of radio ratings data) rates the top five as WLTW-FM, WSKQ-FM, WHTZ-FM, WPAT-FM, andWRKS-FM. Notably, two are Spanish-speaking and one plays an urban format. Sirius Satellite Radio is also located in New York City.

The performing arts scene in New York depends heavily on tourism, an industry that attracted 41.4 million visitors to the city in 2005. Hotel occupancy is at 87.1 percent, the highest in ten years. With pro-arts mayor Michael Bloomberg at the helm, city funding for the arts is getting a boost. It is speculated that when the Dance Theatre of Harlem closed its school in 2005, the large anonymous donation that helped it reopen was a personal donation from the mayor.

And for those sports enthusiasts who dream of turning their passion into their livelihood, the Big Apple is home to Major League Baseball, the National Baseball Association, the National Football League, and the National Hockey League, not to mention the many sports teams that the city hosts. And soon, betting on these teams may become legal. If City Council Member Tony Avella gets his way, legalized sports betting will fund education to the tune of $1.9 billion in new revenue.

The entertainment and sports field generates employment for entertainers, artists, and athletes, but also for talent agents (in sports as well as entertainment), public relations folks, and the requisite managers and accountants.

Job Prospects

Keep in mind that this is among the most competitive industries. Getting a job in sports or entertainment is a difficult undertaking that requires persistence, intense networking, and good luck. Every year, hundreds upon thousands of job seekers flood New York City hoping to become celebrities, and the majority of them wind up waiting tables to make ends meet. And if they decide to stay in show biz, many eventually decide to settle for jobs behind the scenes in production or administration.

Careers in the entertainment industry, regardless of one's previous work experience, usually start at the assistant level; most agents, personal managers, and studio executives gained access this way. Once their careers have been launched, people in the entertainment industry tend to change jobs frequently, and networking is crucial for getting hired.

For those with a business or technical background who don't aspire to make a name for themselves on screen, stage, or the field, work is more readily available. On the management side, people who enter this field are agents, tax or contract lawyers, certified public accountants, or personal finance managers—basically, people who are comfortable with contracts, numbers, large sums of money, and the law.

The big corporations that dominate the industry always need people in the standard management functions: finance, HR, information technology (IT), marketing, and communications. Technicians are needed in traditional fields such as sound engineering and photography and in the rapidly expanding field of digital special effects.

Broadcasting companies need accountants, managers, software developers, and network administrators just like everyone else. A vice president of audience research for Fox Entertainment, for instance, is comparable to a vice president of marketing in another industry. A senior research analyst is simply a market research job specialized for television.

Key Entertainment and Sports Jobs

Key Job	Median NYC Salary ($)	Average Entry-Level NYC Salary ($)
Producer/director	74,110	38,210
Camera operator	40,850	28,530
Multimedia artist/animator	51,710	36,570
Choreographer	100,160	33,600
Music director/composer	37,360	32,350
Radio/TV announcer	50,980	16,660
Sound engineering technician	44,470	25,810
Video editor	45,590	28,650
Set and exhibit designer	54,950	35,440
Actor	Minimum union daily rate: $716*	
	Minimum weekly for Broadway: $1,422	
	Minimum weekly for off-Broadway: $493	
Stage director	$2,500–8,000 for 3/4 week production run	
Orchestra musician	$734–1,925 per contract week	

*As of October 2005
Sources: New York State Department of Labor; WetFeet research

Key NYC Entertainment and Sports Organizations

Organization	2005 Revenue ($M)	1-Yr. Change (%)	Employees	Website
News Corp.	23,859	16.7	44,000	www.newscorp.com
Sony of America	22,331	–7.1	27,000	www.sony.com
NBC Universal	14,689	14.0	21,164	www.nbcuni.com
CBS	14,536	–35.5	38,350	www.cbscorporation.com
ABC	13,207	12.1	22,175	abc.com
Viacom	9,610	n/a	9,500	www.viacom.com
Universal Music Group	5,795	–14.9	1,234	www.umusic.com
Major League Baseball*	4,100	7.9	n/a	www.mlb.com
Warner Music Group	3,502	98.0	4,000	www.wmg.com
National Hockey League*	2,100	5.2	200	www.nhl.com
Columbia House Co.**	1,000	–16.7	2,200	www.columbiahouse.com
Madison Square Garden	804	3.3	n/a	www.thegarden.com
Scientific Games Corp.	782	7.7	3,550	www.scientificgames.com
Marvel Entertainment	391	–24.0	230	www.marvel.com
Town Sports International*	353	3.1	7,440	www.mysportsclubs.com
New York Yankees*	315	32.4	130	www.yankees.com
Bad Boy Worldwide Entertainment Group	300	n/a	600	www.badboyonline.com
Sirius Satellite Radio	242	262.0	514	www.sirius.com
New York Knickerbockers*	170	6.3	22	www.nyknicks.com
New York Football Giants*	154	7.7	62	www.giants.com

*2004 figures

**2003 figures

Source: Hoover's, WetFeet Analysis

Resources

Actors' Equity Association (www.actorsequity.org)

American Federation of Television and Radio Artists (www.aftra.org)

AFTRA New York Local (www.aftra.org/locals/newyork.htm)

American Women in Radio and Television (www.awrt.org)

Billboard (www.billboard.com)

Broadcasting & Cable (www.broadcastingcable.com)

Careers in Entertainment & Sports
(WetFeet Insider Guide, available from www.wetfeet.com)

EntertainmentCareers.net

New York Foundation for the Arts (www.nyfa.org)

Playbill (www.playbill.com)

Recording Industry Association of America (www.riaa.com)

Variety (www.variety.com)

FASHION

New York is the fashion capital of a $172 billion national retail market with sales of $14 billion. But retail is only part of the story—Indeed, the industry defines itself as manufacturing and wholesale apparel sales. During Fashion Week (held each February and September) Bryant Park swarms with celebrities and paparazzi for the unveiling of the latest largely unwearable fashions from famous top designers. To stock stores with the clothes that real people wear, buyers worldwide shop New York's wholesale houses. The city's apparel factories produce 18 percent of all women's outerwear and 28 percent of the dresses made in the United States.

There are 68,000 jobs in fashion-related firms, most of them at businesses with fewer than 20 employees. Apparel manufacturing is the single largest source of manufacturing jobs in the city, and the workforce is predominantly immigrant. In addition, there are eight fashion schools in the city, including the world's largest, the Fashion Institute of Technology.

Manhattan Fashion Industry Employment, 2004*

Industry	Total Firms	Total Employees
Total manufacturing	7,503	118,881
Textile	480	5,228
Apparel	2,035	32,084
Wholesale apparel	3,139	30,929
Total NYC Fashion Industry	**5,654**	**68,241**

*Most recent data available
Source: NYS Department of Labor

Job Prospects

Jobs in the fashion industry are declining at a rate higher than that of the overall manufacturing industry in New York City. In total, fashion industry employment represented only 2.8 percent of Manhattan's total private-sector employment in the fourth quarter of 2004, the lowest percentage ever.

Although fashion design is a creative profession, those who choose this field must be skilled in the use of precision technical plans, blueprints, drawings, and models. Sometimes an entire team of codesigners is needed to turn a lead designer's vision into reality.

Manufacturing jobs are unionized, and hourly workers make close to minimum wage. Garment cutters and sample makers can earn $12 to $25 per hour. Fit models (those with the perfect measurements for standard clothing sizes) work behind the scenes with designers and seamstresses as a merchandise line is developed.

In addition to design, garment production, and sales, a support network has sprung up around fashion, and these businesses can be a source of employment for those interested in breaking into the industry: public relations, event producers, schools, modeling agencies, and fashion magazines such as *Vogue*, *Elle*, *Glamour*, and *Seventeen*.

Key Fashion Jobs

Key Job	Median NYC Salary ($)	Average Entry-Level NYC Salary ($)
Buyer	51,510	34,280
Designer	69,390	45,530
Wholesale sales rep	57,880	33,140
Textile knitters and weavers	21,980	16,860

Sources: New York State Department of Labor; WetFeet research

Key NYC Apparel Companies

Employer	2005 Revenue ($M)	1-Yr. Change (%)	Employees	Website
Liz Claiborne	4,848	4.6	15,400	www.lizclaiborne.com
Polo Ralph Lauren	3,305	24.7	12,762	www.polo.com
AnnTaylor Stores	2,073	11.8	14,900	www.anntaylor.com
Tommy Hilfiger	1,781	–5.1	5,800	www.tommy.com
Coach	1,710	29.5	5,700	www.coach.com
Phillips-Van Heusen*	1,641	5.0	9,700	www.pvh.com
The Warnaco Group	1,504	5.6	10,156	www.warnaco.com
Aéropostale	964	33.4	8,484	www.aeropostale.com
Nautica Enterprises**	694	0.2	3,300	www.nautica.com
Donna Karan	663	n/a	n/a	www.donnakaran.com
Kenneth Cole Productions	518	0.3	1,800	www.kennethcole.com
Jordache Enterprises**	500	n/a	n/a	www.jordachecorporate.com
FUBU**	385	n/a	70	www.fubu.com
Steven Madden	376	11.2	1,414	www.stevemadden.com
Phat Fashions	250	25.0	n/a	www.phatfarm.com
G-III Apparel Group	214	–4.4	384	www.g-iii.com
Eileen Fisher	190	n/a	596	www.eileenfisher.com
Amerex Group Inc.	200	n/a	110	www.amerexgroup.com
Carole Hochman Designs	156	n/a	319	www.carolehochman.com
Prada USA	60.3	–59.8	475	www.prada.com

*2004 figures
**2003 figures (most recent available)
Sources: *Crain's New York Business Times Book of Lists 2006*; Hoover's; WetFeet analysis

Resources

Council of Fashion Designers of America (www.cfda.com)

Fashion Windows (www.fashionwindows.com)

Infomat (www.infomat.com)

SoWear (www.sowear.com)

Women's Wear Daily (www.wwd.com)

FINANCE AND INSURANCE

The U.S. financial market is the largest in the world (and New York City is its capital), but it is gradually losing ground to global competition. In particular, retail savings and investment have experienced low growth. But 2005 was the year of the comeback for financial services. Many industry employers who downsized dramatically in 2002 and 2003 have replenished their headcounts, and their market-based bonuses in 2005 set new records. That's to be expected in an industry sector closely tied to the fluctuations of the stock market. Considering that from 1995 to 2000, the securities industry created 34,000 new jobs, then lost them all, the experts say the overall trend (minus market spikes) is downward. Therefore, expect additional streamlining of services and that profitability will continue to be a focus in this sector. Mergers and consolidations continue to cause reshuffling in competitive rankings. Some of the Manhattan-based institutions, including Morgan Stanley, have moved their back-office organizations outside of the city.

As of the second quarter of 2005, the finance and insurance industries accounted for 10.8 percent of the city's total employment, with more than 318,000 workers in its ranks. New York City is home to more than 10,000 finance and insurance firms.

One of the highest paying (and hardest working) industries, finance has jobs available for recent undergraduate and business school graduates. In addition to traditional jobs in corporate finance, mergers and acquisitions, equity and debt sales and trading, and asset management, this industry hires a range of supporting functions such as human resources, IT, and operations.

Special Note for Women: JPMorgan Chase and American Express are among the five best employers for women (New York City Commission on Women's Issues).

Insurance

U.S. insurance companies offer personal and commercial product lines that include basic health/life and property/casualty protection as well as a long list of other coverage types ranging from automobiles to mortgages to insurance for insurance companies (known as *reinsurance*). These products protect customers from losses resulting from illegal actions, medical needs, theft, earthquakes and hurricanes, and a variety of other causes. They also function as financiers, deriving a large part of their revenues from investments. Insurance companies must maintain enormous reserves of capital to back up potential claims obligations. They invest those reserves in stocks, bonds, and real estate in the United States and overseas, providing a huge amount of liquidity to financial markets and making the industry's influence on the national economy far out of proportion to its size.

Major NYC insurance companies include American International Group, MetLife, Prudential Financial, and New York Life.

INSIDER TIP

Four NYC employers are among *Fortune*'s "Best Companies to Work For" (2005):

American Express (financial services)
PricewaterhouseCoopers (accounting)
Ernst & Young (accounting)
Goldman Sachs Group (investment banking)
Plus Hoboken, New Jersey–based publisher John Wiley & Sons

Retail Brokerage

With the tremendous proliferation of 401(k)s, IRAs, and other types of retirement plans during the 1990s, more people than ever before can now be classified as investors, either directly or indirectly. The choices for the small-time investor have never been greater, and they include stocks, bonds, mutual funds, real estate trusts, individually managed accounts, and various alternative investments. There's also a range of venue options available should one have an itch to invest, including traditional full-service firms, discount brokerages, and do-it-yourself online trading.

Securities and Investments

Traditionally, the field of securities and investments has been the domain of a few Wall Street firms. As federal regulations have eased, however, many of the biggest commercial banks, including Bank of America, Citibank, and JPMorgan Chase, have aggressively added investment banking and asset management units to their consumer and business services. For job seekers interested in corporate finance, securities underwriting, and asset management, many of these firms offer an attractive option. Note that the hiring for these positions is frequently done separately from that for corporate and consumer banking.

Nontraditional Options

Increasingly, a number of nonbank entities are offering opportunities to people interested in financial services. Players include credit card companies such as New York–based American Express, credit card issuers such as Capital One and First USA, and credit-reporting agencies such as Experian. Although people who work at these firms are still in the money business, the specific jobs vary greatly, perhaps more widely than jobs at the traditional banks do. In particular, given the volume of transactions that many of these organizations handle, there are excellent opportunities for people with strong technical skills.

Job Prospects

Securities and investment. The MBA Career Services Council says the news is good for this year's batch of MBA grads. Offers in financial services are not only more plentiful than for 2004–05 grads, but the pay is higher as well. That doesn't mean you'll find the competition any less stiff. This field has always held out for the brightest and the best from the top schools in the country. Those who've completed an internship with a bank have the edge.

Insurance. Ongoing consolidation and technology advances will make for only moderate growth in the insurance industry. The BLS projects 8 percent growth between 2002 and 2012, half of the 16 percent growth average for all industries combined.

As internal business processes and client interactions both become increasingly automated, there will be less demand for employees; insurance agents and underwriters are expected to feel the most impact. Adjusters will not be replaced by technology; face-to-face interaction with the customer is key to this job function. And agents who can sell a variety of insurance types or financial services will face much better prospects than traditional insurance agents.

Retail brokerage. During the trading frenzy of the late '90s, virtual brokers such as E-Trade and Ameritrade were the vehicles of choice for the savvy day trader, but since many of those folks are now eating ramen noodles, these companies have experienced serious declines in activity. Investors increasingly appear to be seeking experienced advice and are willing to pay reasonable incremental costs for help in navigating the current turbulent markets. Though the market rebounded in 2004, retail brokerages have focused on keeping a neat bottom line and resisted aggressive hiring. This is due in no small part to the costs associated with training new brokers—analysts estimate that a full-service brokerage pays about $250,000 to train a new broker and that hiring even seasoned brokers costs firms $150,000 a year.

Key Finance and Insurance Jobs

Key Job	Median NYC Salary ($)	Average Entry-Level NYC Salary ($)
Analyst (BA/BS)	75,180	52,190
Associate (MBA)	140,170	86,920
Claims adjuster	54,780	37,510
Insurance sales agent	54,820	26,210
Loan officers	77,200	35,990
Personal financial advisor	84,370	42,330
Securities sales agent	137,440	74,040
Underwriter	72,090	46,430

Special Note: A major income component in financial services is the year-end bonus (not included in salaries above). At year-end, just before bonuses are paid, there isn't much staff turnover. We're told that firms will sometimes offer to buy out the bonus of a candidate they wish to hire away from a competitor.
Sources: New York State Department of Labor; WetFeet research

Resources

American Academy of Actuaries (www.actuary.org)

American Bankers Association (www.aba.com)

*Careers in Asset Management & Retail Brokerage**

*Careers in Investment Banking**

Insurance Journal (www.insurancejournal.com)

*Killer Investment Banking Resumes**

WetFeet Insider Guides to *The Goldman Sachs Group*, *JPMorgan Chase & Co.*, *Merrill Lynch & Co.*, and *Morgan Stanley*.*

*WetFeet Insider Guides are available online from www.wetfeet.com.

Key NYC Finance and Insurance Firms

Firm	2005 Revenue ($M)	1-Yr. Change (%)	Employees	Website
Citigroup	120,318	11.1	307,000	www.citigroup.com
American International Group	108,905	11.1	97,000	www.aig.com
JPMorgan Chase	79,902	40.3	168,847	www.jpmorganchase.com
UBS	76,383	27.6	69,569	www.ubs.com
Deutsche Bank	72,604	19.7	63,427	www.db.com
Morgan Stanley	51,770	30.9	53,218	www.morganstanley.com
Merrill Lynch & Co.	47,783	47.2	54,600	www.ml.com
MetLife	44,776	14.8	65,500	www.metlife.com
The Goldman Sachs Group	43,391	45.4	31,005	www.gs.com
Lehman Brothers Holdings	32,420	52.6	22,900	www.lehman.com
Prudential Financial	31,708	11.9	38,853	www.prudential.com
American Express	24,267	–16.7	65,800	www.americanexpress.com
New York Life Insurance*	17,330	15.5	12,650	www.newyorklife.com
Bear Stearns	11,552	37.2	11,843	www.bearstearns.com
Marsh & McLennan	11,469	–5.7	55,000	www.marshmac.com
TIAA-CREF*	10,864	–15.2	5,700	www.tiaa-cref.org
AXA Financial*	9,645	27.3	11,800	www.axa-financial.com
Assurant	7,497	1.1	12,000	www.assurant.com
Credit Suisse USA	7,025	10.8	10,899	www.csfb.com
Guardian Life Insurance of America*	7,021	4.3	5,000	www.guardianlife.com

*2004 figures
Sources: Hoover's; WetFeet analysis

HEALTH CARE

The health-care industry provides diagnostic, healing, and rehabilitation services for the injured, ailing, incapacitated, and disabled, and preventative services for the healthy. But in New York, a significant part of its role is research. New York hospitals have carved out specialty niches: New York University is known for its epilepsy research, New York Presbyterian for its work in Parkinson's disease, Rockefeller University for its stem cell research, and Mt. Sinai School of Medicine for its work in Alzheimer's. In 2006, Columbia University announced plans to build a neuroscience research center to study brain diseases and childhood development disorders and New York-Presbyterian Hospital/Columbia University Medical Center is building a new heart center.

While the individual physician is the industry's first line of contact with consumers, the health-care organization—the hospital or health management organization (HMO)—is the conduit of insurance payments, which control the industry's, and the physician's, revenue. The lion's share of this revenue comes from employee health insurance plans, Medicare (health insurance for Americans over 65), and Medicaid (health insurance for Americans on welfare). Empire Blue Cross is the insurer of choice in New York City with twice the members of Aetna, number two on the list. But the real runner-up, if you count by overall member numbers, is UnitedHealthcare and its subsidiary Oxford Health.

The health-care industry overall is marked by inflationary costs and it's no different in New York. New York-Presbyterian is the largest hospital and thus spends the most. Saint Vincent's, which operates seven New York hospitals, is in bankruptcy: In the last year it has closed St. Mary's in Brooklyn and a hospital on Staten Island, trimming 1,000 jobs. As the U.S. population ages, growing shortages of qualified workers are predicted. Hospitals have the highest unfilled job rates in this industry. Pharmacists, radiological technologists, billing coders, laboratory technologists, registered nurses, and housekeeping and maintenance workers are in demand. Part of the hospital workforce shortage is due to an increase in the range of employment options (and higher salaries) in health care outside hospitals. Because of the diversity of the city's population, health-care workers are often required to speak more than one language.

Job Prospects

Health services is the largest industry in New York, with 525,375 jobs and 18,365 employers. Among the jobs for which there are the most openings projected between 2002 and 2012 are nurses, personal and home care aides, home health aides, nursing aides, orderlies, and attendants. Although specialized training is required for most medical professions, there is demand for health-care administrators with master's degrees and patient services coordinators with bachelor's degrees, who ensure quality patient care while protecting the institution from liability. Technical and administrative support positions are in high demand as the health-care industry evolves in a competitive market. Health-care IT is a steadily growing sector, due to the industry's relative lack of IT investment thus far.

Key Health-Care Jobs

Key Job	Median NYC Salary ($)	Average Entry-Level NYC Salary($)
Dietician	48,850	40,190
Family practitioner	124,230	60,090
Internist	145,600+	n/a
Medical technician	39,980	30,880
Pharmacist	87,650	67,030
Physical therapist	66,680	50,240
Physician assistant	75,350	58,530
Registered nurse	71,400	54,780
Veterinarian	83,860	41,890
Dental hygienist	66,120	55,040

Note: These positions often require specialized training in addition to an undergraduate degree.
Sources: New York State Department of Labor; WetFeet research

Key NYC Hospitals

Hospital	2004 Operating Expenses ($M)	Employees	Website
New York–Presbyterian Hospital	2,405	15,572	www.nyp.org
Montefiore Medical Center	1,734	10,933	www.montefiore.org
Memorial Sloan-Kettering Cancer Center	1,158	6,702	www.mskcc.org
North Shore University Hospital Manhasset	1,104	5,444	www.northshorelij.com
Beth Israel Medical Center	1,084	7,610	www.wehealny.org
Mount Sinai Medical Center	1,055	6,676	www.mountsinai.org
St. Luke's–Roosevelt Hospital Center	918	5,194	www.wehealny.org
Long Island Jewish Medical Center	911	4,950	www.northshorelij.com
Saint Vincent Catholic Medical Centers (Brooklyn & Queens)	691	4,348	www.svcmc.org
NYU Medical Center	690	5,086	www.nyumedicalcenter.org
Maimonides Medical Center	621	5,064	www.maimonidesmed.org
St. Vincent's Hospital Manhattan	568	3,804	www.svcmc.org
Lenox Hill Hospital	520	3,004	www.lenoxhillhospital.org
Bellevue Hospital Center	513	4,641	www.nyc.gov/html/hhc/home.html
Kings County Hospital Center	502	4,856	www.nyc.gov/html/hhc/home.html
Bronx-Lebanon Hospital Center	451	3,607	www.bronxcare.org
New York Methodist	448	2,855	www.nym.org
Jacobi Medical Center	447	3,717	www.nyc.gov/html/hhc/home.html
Saint Barnabas Medical Center	432	3,350	www.saintbarnabas.com
New York Hospital Medical Center of Queens	415	2,830	www.nyhq.org

Source: *Crain's New York City Book of Lists 2006*

Key NYC Health Organizations

Health Insurers	2004 Revenue ($M)	Employees	Website
Empire Blue Cross Blue Shield, WellChoice*	5,827	5,500	www.wellchoice.com
Aetna**	22,492	28,200	www.aetna.com
GHI**	2,148	2,000	www.ghi.com
Health Insurance Plan of Greater New York	3,654	3,000	www.hipusa.com
Oxford Health Plans	n/a	3,500	www.oxhp.com
United Healthcare Insurance	8,653	30,000	www.uhc.com
CIGNA	16,684	32,700	www.cigna.com
Healthfirst	577	n/a	www.healthfirstny.com
Health Plus	509	n/a	www.healthplus-ny.org
MetroPlus Health Plan	207	n/a	www.metroplus.org
Other Health Organizations			
Quest Diagnostics**	5,504	41,500	www.questdiagnostics.com
BioScrip Inc.**	1,073	974	www.bioscrip.com
National Medical Health Card Systems**	801	484	www.nmhcs.com
Allied Healthcare International**	351	980	www.alliedhealthcare.com
HMS Holdings**	60.0	331	www.hmsholdings.com
Schick Technologies**	52.4	139	www.schicktech.com
New York Health Care**	48.9	1,929	www.nyhc.com
NWH**	19.4	184	www.nwhinc.com

*2003 figures

**2005 figures

Sources: *Crain's New York Business Book of Lists 2006*; Hoover's; WetFeet analysis

Resources

American Medical Association (www.ama-assn.org)

Health News Digest (www.healthnewsdigest.com)

New York Academy of Medicine (www.nyam.org)

New York City Department for the Aging (www.ci.nyc.ny.us/html/dfta/home.html)

New York State Department of Health (www.health.state.ny.us)

WetFeet's Health Care Industry Profile (www.wetfeet.com)

HOSPITALITY AND FOOD SERVICE

Gas prices may be outrageous, but that hasn't kept tourists away from The Big Apple. Forty-one million of them arrived in 2005, occupying 85 percent of the city's hotel rooms and nudging the average room rate to $243 per night.

The biggest change in the travel industry in recent years has been the rise of the Internet. Rather than use a travel agent, it is now possible to research destinations and compare prices yourself by visiting websites that provide all that information in one place. If you're looking for a job as a travel agent or reservations clerk, you might want to rethink your career plan. On the other hand, you might consider a job in the hotel industry. Manhattan added 12 new hotels in 2005 with 2,200 new rooms, raising the total Manhattan room count to more than 72,700.

As in many other industries, the big players in the hospitality and tourism industry have become vastly more efficient due to technology and management advances. How can smaller hotels, motels, and tour operators compete with bigger players who pay half what they do for supplies? For many, the answer is finding a market niche that is not adequately served by the big players (gay or lesbian cruises, Jewish-focused tours of Jerusalem, etc.). But many of these companies will be so small that they'll rarely have an open position for you to fill.

Job Prospects

The New York tourism bureau reports that tourism generates $12 billion in wages and supports over 325,000 jobs in all five boroughs. The city plans to add nearly 5,000 new or renovated hotel rooms to its current inventory of more than 72,700 by the end of 2007. New York City closed 2005 with 22 million room nights booked, an increase of 600,000 room nights over 2004. The trend is toward developing boutique hotels, less expensive hotels, and hotels in diverse locations such as Harlem, Brooklyn, Queens, Staten Island, the Lower East Side, and Tribeca. U.S. hotels are shrinking in size, with most offering 75 or fewer rooms, and the trend is away from luxury hotels to mid-scale and limited-service brands.

And it only takes a glance down New York City's streets to reveal the gradual disappearance of independently owned cafes in favor of Starbucks and Cosi chains. Food service and drinking establishments were affected by 9/11, but have since rebounded. And for those who prefer to stay in, online grocer FreshDirect will deliver dinner makings to your door.

You'll find the usual array of corporate positions within the hospitality and tourism industry: marketing executives, salespeople, accountants, HR specialists, and the like. But the majority of career opportunities in the industry are in customer service–oriented jobs.

Key Hospitality Jobs

Key Job	Median NYC Salary ($)	Average Entry-Level NYC Salary ($)
Food service manager	48,550	34,710
General manager	129,140	70,680
Lodging manager	67,770	44,880
Meeting and convention planner	50,400	38,390
Purchasing agent	59,980	41,090
Travel agent	34,190	22,060
Flight attendant	39,470	23,890
Tour guide	24,310	17,260
Housekeeping manager	41,730	27,940
Chef or head cook	43,480	30,770
Waiter or waitress	23,460	18,010

Sources: New York State Department of Labor; WetFeet research

Resources

Hospitality Net (www.hospitalitynet.org)

New York State Hospitality & Tourism Association (www.nyshta.org)

Travel Industry Association of America (www.tia.org)

Key NYC Hospitality and Food Service Organizations

Organization	NYC Employees	Website
Triarc Companies	5,360	www.triarc.com
Charmer Sunbelt Group	3,000	www.charmer-sunbelt.com
Loews Hotels	2,100	www.loewshotels.com
Riese Organization	2,000	www.rieserestaurants.com
Ark Restaurants	2,038	www.arkrestaurants.com
Waldorf-Astoria	1,659	www.waldorf.com
Fresh Direct	1,500	www.freshdirect.com
Hilton New York	1,453	www.newyorktowers.hilton.com
New York Marriott Marquis	1,900	www.nymarriottmarquis.com
Manhattan Beer Distributors	1,200	www.manhattanbeer.com
Sheraton New York Hotel and Towers	1,100	www.sheraton.com
New York Palace Hotel	1,000	www.newyorkpalace.com
Grand Hyatt New York	959	www.grandnewyork.hyatt.com
Peerless Importers Inc	800	www.peerimp.com
The Roosevelt Hotel	580	www.therooseveltthotel.com
Hotel Pennsylvania	465	www.hotelpenn.com
New York Helmsley	430	www.helmsleyhotels.com
JetBlue Airways	420	www.jetblue.com
Milford Plaza Hotel	368	www.milfordplaza.com
Nebraskaland	152	www.nebraskaland.com

Source: *Crain's New York Books of Lists 2006*

LAW

Nearly every U.S. law firm with a national presence has a strong NYC practice, and a number of the nation's largest firms are headquartered here. Although the NYC law industry's size is promising for legal hopefuls, the city's practices are not experiencing significant growth.

No longer can you plan to step directly from law school into the partnership track of a large firm. The trend is for the mega-practices to cut back on the number of vested partners. To keep revenue ahead of costs, firms have increased the ratio of associates to partners from one-to-one to five partners for every six associates. Paralegals now do the work previously assigned to associates, and "career attorneys" stay on at salaries higher than other associates, but have little or no chance of making partner.

Like doctors, lawyers have many specialties. Two main categories of private-sector lawyers are transactional (corporate) lawyers and litigators. Transactional lawyers deal with a wide range of business issues: corporate financing, contracts, acquisitions, bankruptcy, and others. The goal of this work is to get deals done and avoid future legal problems. New York City is one of the country's major transaction-law centers. Litigators, on the other hand, deal with legal problems after they occur. Litigators handle issues that could land their clients in court: breaches of contract, securities-law problems, rogue trading, class-action suits, antitrust actions, employment-related problems, and the like. They are found in every city, but especially in New York and Washington, D.C. Other specialties include intellectual property, tax, real estate, labor and employment, environmental, personal injury, and family law, to name a few.

Job Prospects

New York City has the highest concentration of lawyers in the country: Upward of 55,000 after 10,843 new positions were reported by the city's law firms in 2005. Your best chances are with smaller firms, where the biggest growth is now occurring. And some of the fastest growing are out-of-town firms with offices in New York City.

Job placement following law school remains high, because legal skills are used in many fields—only 58 percent of law graduates are now employed by law firms. In fact, the lawyers who make the most money work as talent agents/managers or with oil or computer companies. Others hang out their own shingles and represent individuals or small companies in divorces, bankruptcies, or estate planning. Still others work for the government, in various agencies or as district attorneys or public defenders, or for advocacy groups such as the ACLU or the NAACP. There are even people who, although technically lawyers because they've gone to law school and passed the bar exam, do not practice law, working instead in business, banking, academia, or politics. The industry employs high-caliber support people, known as paralegals, who do everything from word processing to legal research. Fewer opportunities exist for arbitrators/mediators, court reporters, judges, and law clerks.

Key Law Jobs

Key Job	Median NYC Salary ($)	Average Entry-Level NYC Salary ($)
Arbitrator	68,190	50,590
Court reporter	80,610	52,560
Law clerk	39,500	30,710
Lawyer	130,440	71,410
Law firm associate	n/a	125,000
Paralegal	48,320	34,700

Sources: New York State Department of Labor; WetFeet research

Key NYC Law Firms

Law Firm	NY Area Lawyers	Total NY Area Staff	Website
Skadden, Arps, Slate, Meagher & Flom	768	1,719	www.skadden.com
Simpson Thacher & Bartlett	638	1,391	www.simpsonthacher.com
Paul, Weiss, Rifkind, Wharton & Garrison	604	1,365	www.paulweiss.com
Weil, Gotshal & Manges	562	1,358	www.weil.com
Davis Polk & Wardwell	502	1,262	www.dpw.com
Shearman & Sterling	486	1,211	www.shearman.com
Proskauer Rose	485	1,091	www.proskauer.com
Cravath Swaine & Moore	468	1,324	www.cravath.com
Debevoise & Plimpton	450	1,162	www.debevoise.com
Wilson, Elser, Moskowitz, Edelman & Dicker	448	n/a	www.wemed.com
Cleary, Gottlieb, Steen & Hamilton	440	1,262	www.cgsh.com
Clifford Chance US	421	933	www.cliffordchance.com
White & Case	417	1,083	www.whitecase.com
Sidley Austin Brown & Wood	409	769	www.sidley.com
Sullivan & Cromwell	407	1,292	www.sullcrom.com
Schulte Roth & Zabel	399	612	www.srz.com
Cadwalader, Wickersham & Taft	389	n/a	www.cadwalader.com
Willkie Farr & Gallagher	386	901	www.willkie.com
Fried, Frank, Harris, Shriver, & Jacobson	364	n/a	www.friedfrank.com
Kaye Scholer	353	n/a	www.kayescholer.com
Dewey Ballantine	343	n/a	www.deweyballantine.com

Source: *Crain's New York Book of Lists 2006*

Resources

American Bar Association (www.abanet.org)

Association of the Bar of the City of New York (www.abcny.org)

FindLaw (www.findlaw.com)

Law.com

New York Law Journal (www.law.com/jsp/nylj/index.jsp)

New York Lawyer (www.nylawyer.com)

New York State Trial Lawyers Association (www.nystla.org)

New York State Bar Association (www.nysba.org)

MANAGEMENT CONSULTING

With Accenture and McKinsey headquartered here, not to mention a world-class array of potential corporate clients, New York City offers some of the best strategy consulting opportunities in the world. Even the city itself is an occasional consulting client: Accenture helped New York initiate its 311 call center, where you can get free information in 170 languages on topics as diverse as how to dispose of a dead cat, how to collect unemployment payments, and how much to tip your building super. (During the August 2003 blackout, 311 fielded 150,000 calls in two days.)

Consulting firms grew at double-digit rates throughout the 1990s, but ever since, the industry's growth has been slow, with declining revenues—and morale—at many of the top consulting firms. Firms are hiring, but growth is in the single digits and competition for jobs is fierce, so prepare carefully. Know why you want to be a consultant, know why you want to work at the firms you're applying to, dot all your *i*s, and cross all your *t*s.

One of the reasons for slow growth is that many client companies have hired former consultants as employees, bringing their expertise in-house and reducing reliance on outside firms. Also there is a trend to hire industry experts rather than the newly graduated MBAs the firms used to acquire in droves. The focus on cost-cutting and caution regarding IT and other spending chipped away at the availability of consulting work. Fee growth has generally been flat since 2001. Outsourcing, which transfers activities from a company to a consulting firm, provides stable margins, but doesn't create more jobs for consultants.

Job Prospects

Large consulting firms hire undergraduates and MBAs from top business schools or recruit specialists directly from the competition or from the industry. Opportunities also exist with small firms, boutiques, and sole proprietorships that are composed of technical specialists such as information technologists or marketing consultants. The fastest growing segments of this market are systems analysis and administrative services.

Although the competition at elite firms is especially intense, the qualities that all recruiters look for are similar: Besides outstanding academic records, they want people who are problem solvers, creative thinkers, good communicators, and who have a keen understanding of and interest in business. Top candidates will also have previous experience in the business world (consulting internships are impressive but not required) and a record of extracurricular achievement. Companies specializing in IT consulting or e-business may require technical skills and experience.

Most firms offer internships to highly qualified undergraduates. Competition for internships can be even more intense than for permanent positions, but a successful internship can dramatically increase a candidate's chances of getting an offer after graduation.

Key Consulting Jobs

Key Job	Median NYC Salary ($)	Average Entry-Level NYC Salary($)
Actuary	106,970	69,030
Administrative services manager	89,150	62,580
Database administrator	79,760	51,360
Analyst (BA/BS)	72,150	48,240
Associate (MBA)	n/a	100,000–130,000

Sources: New York State Department of Labor; WetFeet research

Resources

*Careers in Management Consulting**

Consulting Central (www.consultingcentral.com)

Consulting Magazine (www.consultingmag.com)

Institute of Management Consultants USA (www.imcusa.org)

*Killer Consulting Resumes**

McKinsey Quarterly (www.mckinseyquarterly.com)

*Specialized Consulting Careers: Health Care, Human Resources, and Information Technology**

WetFeet Insider Guides to *Accenture, Deloitte Consulting*, and *McKinsey & Company**

*WetFeet Insider Guides are available online at www.wetfeet.com.

Key NYC Management Consulting Firms

Firm	2005 Revenue ($M)	1-Yr. Growth (%)	NYC Consultants	Website
Accenture	17,094	13.1	2,571	www.accenture.com
Aon Corp.	9,837	–3.3	436	www.aon.com
Mercer	3,802	4.5	700	www.mercer.com
Deloitte Consulting**	3,245	3.0	n/a	www.deloitte.com
McKinsey & Co.**	3,000	0.0	n/a	www.mckinsey.com
Capgemini U.S.*	1,911	–16.6	100	www.capgemini.com
Towers Perrin*	1,620	8	275	www.towersperrin.com
Mercer HR Consulting	852	290.4	345	www.mercerhr.com
A.T. Kearney**	846	–15.8	300	www.atkearney.com
Watson Wyatt & Co.	737	5.0	240	www.watsonwyatt.com
Roland Berger Strategy Consultants*	723	4.5	20	www.rolandberger.com
USI Holdings Corp	499	22.9	51	www.usi.biz
Milliman USA**	348	7.7	120	www.milliman.com
Kurt Salmon Associates**	132	9.1	60	www.kurtsalmon.com
Eisner	82.1	12.2	n/a	www.eisnerllp.com
The Segal Group**	60.6	n/a	237	www.segalco.com
Protiviti*	41.4	–68.9	70	www.protiviti.com
Mercer Oliver Wyman	33.2	n/a	150	www.merceroliverwyman.com

*2004 figure
**2003 figures
Sources: *Crain's New York Business Book of Lists 2006*; Hoover's; WetFeet analysis

MANUFACTURING

Once an industrial center, Manhattan has transformed itself into a service economy and bid farewell to many manufacturing companies that left the city in search of more affordable real estate. Yet many prominent names remain and others are housed in nearby communities, like PepsiCo, which has its headquarters up the Hudson River in Purchase, New York; aerospace company Curtiss-Wright Corp. in Roseland, New Jersey; AEP, which makes plastic products in Hackensack, New Jersey; and Bellco Health, which makes medical supplies in North Amityville, New York.

In Queens, the College Point Corporate Park is becoming a haven for printing companies. ARES Printing & Packaging and Inland Paper Products have operations there. But for the most part, today's product manufacturers with New York addresses are multinational corporations located in slick high-rise office buildings: Altria, Dover Corporation, Philips Electronics. It's unlikely you'll actually see an assembly line or production floor, let alone a smokestack-spouting factory. Rather, Manhattan is a bastion for those who make the deals and file the financials, while production itself takes place elsewhere—as in all over the world.

More recently, the city has become a center for the biotech and pharmaceutical sector. One of the most prestigious new development projects is the East River Science Park. The new 872,000-square-foot commercial bioscience center is expected to attract the world's leading health-care and pharmaceutical companies, creating more than 2,000 jobs and a $350 million annual economic impact. Pfizer, the largest drug company in the world, has headquarters in New York City, as does Bristol-Myers Squibb. Schering-Plough is headquartered in Kenilworth, New Jersey.

New York's famous fashion and beauty industry has spawned a number of prominent cosmetic companies. If today they seem fewer in number (Avon, Revlon, Estée Lauder) than what you see represented in your local department store, it's because the few have acquired the many. Estée Lauder, for example, owns Aramis, Clinique, Prescriptives,

Origins, MAC, Bobbi Brown, Donna Karan, Aveda, La Mer, Stila, Bumble and Bumble, Kate Spade Beauty, Darphin, Michael Kors, Rodan + Fields, American Beauty, Flirt!, and Good Skin. Whew, that's a mouthful! (In this book, apparel manufacturers are discussed in the "Fashion" section, earlier in this chapter.)

Job Prospects

Professional job opportunities include finance, accounting, real estate management, sales, customer service, and market research and development (R&D). And constantly emerging new products and increasing competition promise to provide positions for brand managers and marketers from now until the end of time. Senior management positions in marketing, operations, R&D, and other departments tend to be filled from within, or by professionals who have already worked in the industry. Manufacturing tends to be a hierarchical business and though merit and hard work count for a lot, even the wunderkinds have to do time before they're promoted.

The mammoth companies often recruit on campus and boast strong training programs for recent college grads, but they're also known to pull experienced people from other firms in their industry. If you choose to remain in manufacturing for a long time—and many people do—you can spend time overseas, try out new products and categories, and ultimately move into general management.

On the downside, there are areas in the industry with less-certain futures. Technology is sure to eliminate lots of workers, as functions such as production, packaging, and customer service become increasingly automated or migrate overseas to cheaper labor pools.

Key Manufacturing Jobs

Key Jobs	Median NYC Salary ($)	Average Entry-Level NYC Salary($)
General and operations managers	129,140	70,680
Sales managers	142,940	85,250
Biochemist/biophysicist	54,710	40,770
Lab tech	38,740	29,330
Biomedical engineer	62,070	46,860
Chemical engineer	73,860	66,090
Engineering manager	113,040	79,100
First line supervisor	52,290	29,120
Human resources managers, all other	91,190	67,370
Market research analyst	59,800	39,850
Marketing managers	132,310	78,370
Materials engineer	68,510	60,230
Occupational health and safety engineer	65,080	46,450
Production manager	96,030	65,920
Purchasing agent	59,980	41,090
Sales representative	56,170	40,870
Distribution manager	81,790	58,440
Industrial engineer	78,200	53,920

Sources: New York State Department of Labor; WetFeet research

Key NYC Manufacturing Firms

Firm	2005 Revenue ($M)	1-Yr. Change (%)	NYC Employees	Website
Altria Group	68,920	7.7	1,400	www.altria.com
Pfizer	51,298	–2.3	2,500	www.pfizer.com
Bristol-Myers Squibb	19,207	–0.9	1,200	www.bms.com
Colgate-Palmolive	11,397	7.7	3,000	www.colgate.com
Philips Electronics North America*	10,159	2.3	150	www.usa.philips.com
L-3 Communications	9,445	36.9	100	www.l-3com.com
Avon Products	8,150	5.2	250	www.avoncompany.com
The Estée Lauder Companies	6,336	9.4	1,000	www.elcompanies.com
Dover	6,078	10.8	20	www.dovercorporation.com
Forest Laboratories**	2,912	–6.5	227	www.frx.com
Tiffany & Co.**	2,395	8.6	1,200	www.tiffany.com
Sequa Corp.	1,998	7.2	80	www.sequa.com
NBTY	1,737	5.2	861	www.nbty.com
Revlon	1,332	2.7	40	www.revloninc.com
Standard Motor Products	830	0.7	4,100	www.smpcorp.com
National Envelope	650	1.6	n/a	www.nationalenvelope.com
EDO	649	20.9	2,546	www.edocorp.com

*2004 figures
**2006 figures
Sources: *Crains New York Business Book of Lists 2006*; Hoover's; WetFeet analysis

Resources

American Society for Quality (www.asq.org)

Biotechnology Industry Organization (www.bio.org)

New York Biotechnology Association (www.BioNY.org)

*Careers in Biotech & Pharmaceuticals**

*Careers in Consumer Products**

*Careers in Manufacturing**

Manufacturing.net

National Association of Manufacturers (www.nam.org)

New York Biotechnology Association (www.nyba.org)

Pharmaceutical Research and Manufacturers of America (www.phrma.org)

*WetFeet Insider Guides are available online at www.wetfeet.com.

PUBLISHING

With offices for 200 newspapers and 350 consumer magazines, New York is the undisputed publishing capital of the world. Consolidation and vertical integration have changed not only who owns what, but also how business is done. For instance, Time Warner hedges its bets with both Internet and print, owning AOL as well as Time Inc., and retailer Barnes & Noble now also publishes books under its own imprint. Rupert Murdoch's News Corporation owns Fox Entertainment as well as MySpace.com. The *New York Times* recently purchased About.com. In fact the Internet is the not-so-new story of publishing. The e-book may have bombed, but let's face it, it's easier to sneak a peek at the news online than read a newspaper at your desk. The Internet has also changed the way people advertise and promote. One of the most discussed pubs on the block is an e-newsletter, *Daily Candy*, started by Dany Levy, an enterprising former *New York Magazine* staffer. The whole thing is about product promotion and the asking price is a cool $100 million.

Newspapers employ the most workers, and several large corporations, including the NYC-based Hearst Corp. and the *New York Times*, own most of the newspapers in the country. Book publishing is also dominated by a few very large companies, most of which are based in New York City. Textbooks and technical, scientific, and professional books provide nearly half of the revenue of the book publishing industry. Technical publishers, such as Addison-Wesley, also tend to cluster in New York.

The publishing industry produces magazines, books, newspapers, directories, greeting cards, databases, and calendars, and material in other formats, such as audio, CD-ROM, and other electronic media as well. Many mass-market magazines such as *Time*, *The New Yorker*, *Rolling Stone*, and *Vanity Fair* are published in New York City. So are many of the special-interest magazines published by outfits such as Hachette Filipacchi (*Woman's Day*, *Elle*, *Car and Driver*, and *Metropolitan Home*).

Job Prospects

Budding Lois Lanes may find it tough to get a start in the competitive publishing marketplace. New graduates should consider apprenticeships and internships as a way to break into the field. Growth in traditional publishing jobs is projected to decline by 1 percent through 2012 (while overall employment growth over the same period is expected to be 16 percent). That doesn't mean fewer books, newspapers, and magazines will be produced, but efficiencies in production and an increase in the use of freelance writers will keep employment from increasing. One demand that is expected to increase is for writers who cover subjects appealing to growing minority populations.

There are many publishing jobs in editorial, design, and photography, but opportunities also exist for sales, marketing, and public relations professionals. Major book publishers often have large warehouse operations.

Insider Tip: Taking Columbia University's summer publishing course is a great way to get a job. It's pricey, but those who've enrolled say it's well worth the commitment. Those who take it make the right contacts.

Special Note for Women: Time Warner is among the five best employers for women in New York City (Source: New York City Commission on Women's Issues).

Key Publishing Jobs

Key Jobs	Median NYC Salary ($)	Average Entry-Level NYC Salary($)
Advertising sales	56,960	36,430
Art director	90,790	54,570
Writer	57,260	35,580
Editor	57,720	35,300
Graphic artist	53,490	32,100
Reporter	52,570	30,750

Sources: New York State Department of Labor; WetFeet research

Resources

American Association of Publishers (www.publishers.org)

Council of Literary Magazines and Presses (www.clmp.org)

Editor & Publisher (www.editorandpublisher.com)

Magazine Publishers of America (www.magazine.org)

Media Bistro (www.mediabistro.com)

New York Times Media & Advertising section (www.nytimes.com/pages/business/media)

Publishers Marketplace (www.publishersmarketplace.com)

Publishers Weekly (www.publishersweekly.com)

Online Journalism Review (www.ojr.org)

Key NYC Publishing Companies

Company	2005 Revenue ($M)	1-Yr. Change (%)	NYC Employees	Website
Time Warner	43,652	3.7	500	www.timewarner.com
The McGraw-Hill Companies	6,004	14.3	750	www.mcgraw-hill.com
Advance Publications	5,276	n/a	n/a	www.advance.net
The Hearst Corp.*	4,000	–2.4	2,500	www.hearstcorp.com
Bloomberg*	3,500	7.7	n/a	www.bloomberg.com
The New York Times Co.	3,373	2.1	350	www.nytco.com
Random House	2,443	9.6	1,900	www.randomhouse.com
Scholastic Corp.	2.080	–6.9	9	www.scholastic.com
Dow Jones & Co.	1,770	5.9	500	www.dj.com
Thomson Financial	1,734	13.5	1,000	www.thomson.com/financial
Kaplan*	1,135	35.4	5	www.kaplan.com
Primedia	991	–24.2	90	www.primedia.com
John Wiley & Sons	974	5.5	3,400	www.wiley.com
Advanstar Communications*	381	16.8	1,400	www.advanstar.com
Topps Company**	294	–0.7	483	www.topps.com
Martha Stewart Living Omnimedia	210	11.8	300	www.marthastewart.com
VNU Business Media	170	n/a	1,500	www.vnu.com
AMREP	133	4.1	70	www.amrepcorp.com
Princeton Review	131	–3.5	200	www.princetonreview.com
iVillage	91.1	36.2	215	www.ivillage.com

*2004 figures
**2006 figures
Sources: Hoover's; WetFeet analysis

REAL ESTATE

Ever since John Jacob Astor traded in his empire of beaver pelts for a gamble on uptown Manhattan real estate, real estate speculation has created some of America's greatest fortunes. New York City is coming back from the exodus that followed 9/11, with major building projects underway not only around the World Trade Center site, but throughout Lower Manhattan, Harlem, downtown Brooklyn, and the city's waterfront areas.

And in the continuing story of the rich getting richer, *Crain's New York Business* reports that the largest New York property managers now control 50 percent of the city's commercial footage. The average going rate is $43.20 per square foot and projections are that it will reach $90 by 2010. Vacancies are at 8.4 percent.

The average price of a Manhattan condo or co-op is $1.3 million. And that cute townhouse in the West Village? Only $5.8 million. But rising mortgage rates are starting to cool this hot market. Bloomberg.com reports that sales fell 1.1 percent during the first quarter of 2006 and a record number of owners panicked and put their places up for sale. The number of apartments on the market rose 60 percent to 6,904. All of this makes for a grand opportunity for realtors.

Real estate is a cyclical industry affected by economic boons and banes, but the lows in New York City are still higher than in most cities. If you've worked in real estate in other places, you'll have some catching up to do here in terms of laws and regulations. And you'll have to learn not to blink an eye when you deliver your first counter-offer and announce that your client simply can't accept any less for his one-bedroom place than $1.3 million.

Job Prospects

Real estate jobs and the construction industry are symbiotic in terms of job opportunities for brokers, agents, and property managers. As the city's inventory of commercial and residential buildings increases, so will the jobs for those who sell, rent, and manage them. It also stimulates the janitorial and maintenance sector for folks who do the, uh, dirty work.

There are 5,260 real estate agents in New York City, and 420 brokers. There are also opportunities for property managers. If this is your interest, you'll find the best pay working for a large corporation rather than for a property management company. Pharmaceutical companies, religious organizations, telecommunications firms, and scientific research organizations are all landlords.

Key Real Estate Jobs

Key Jobs	Average NYC Salary ($)	Entry Level ($)
Agent	54,130	32,400
Appraiser	63,190	49,150
Broker	58,850	38,860
Property manager	59,200	43,440
Title examiner	22,860	21,620

Sources: New York State Department of Labor; WetFeet research

Resources

Careers in Real Estate (WetFeet Insider Guide, available from www.wetfeet.com)

Institute of Real Estate Management (www.irem.org)

National Association of Realtors (www.realtor.org)

RealEstateJournal (www.realestatejournal.com)

Realty Times (http://realtytimes.com)

Key NYC Real Estate Companies

Company	2005 Revenue ($M)	1-Yr. Change (%)	NYC Employees	Website
Cendant	18,236	–7.8	350	www.cendant.com
The Trump Organization*	10,400	22.4	100	www.trumponline.com
Vornado Realty Trust	2,809	41.6	186	www.vno.com
Cushman & Wakefield	1,200	9.1	600	www.cushmanwakefield.com
iStar Financial	802	14.9	30	www.istarfinancial.com
Kajima U.S.A.	793	n/a	n/a	www.kajimausa.com
Kimco Realty	773	12.7	452	www.kimcorealty.com
Annaly Mortgage Management	687	25.0	20	www.annaly.com
Tarragon	674	100.7	25	www.tarragoncorp.com
SL Green Realty Corp.	501	20.7	400	www.slgreen.com
New Plan Excel Realty Trust	496	–2.1	131	www.newplanexcel.com
MFA Mortgage Investments	225	24.6	11	www.mfa-reit.com
Lexington Corporate Properties Trust	203	25.8	29	www.lxp.com
W. P. Carey	184	–22.5	6	www.wpcarey.com
Capital Trust	105	82.9	25	www.capitaltrust.com
Silverstein Properties	3.0	n/a	110	www.silversteinproperties.com
Tishman Speyer Properties	n/a	n/a	n/a	www.tishmanspeyer.com
Newmark Knight Frank	n/a	n/a	n/a	www.newmarkre.com

*2004 figures

Sources: *Crain's New York Business Book of Lists 2006*; Hoover's; WetFeet analysis

RETAIL TRADE

New York City is arguably the shopping capital of the nation. You can literally find everything you could want—sometimes all within the same block. From the cut-rate shops selling luggage on Sixth Avenue to the swank of Barneys to the sidewalk vendors on Canal Street, New York has it all.

Department stores, at one time the primary shopping outlet of America, are now being challenged on one end by small boutiques carrying designer wear and on the other by discount powerhouses like H&M and Century 21. To remain competitive, department stores have recently begun upgrading their point-of-sale software.

Another factor to consider is the growth of retail business being conducted online. Leadpile.com predicts sales will hit the big $100 billion in 2006 after totaling $81 billion in 2005. And trend watchers say cross-channel shoppers—consumers who do their shopping online and their buying in stores—influence $125 billion in offline sales.

Job Prospects

Retail is a high-turnover industry—there will always be job openings. According to the New York State Department of Labor, retail salespersons and cashiers are the two top positions with the most openings projected through 2012. Only 2 percent of retail jobs are in management positions such as buyers and department and store managers. Computer technology has reduced some positions in bookkeeping and inventory control, and e-commerce has replaced some of the personal over-the-counter interaction that marks this industry.

Key Retail Jobs

Key Jobs	Median NYC Salary ($)
Buyer	51,740
Demonstrator/product promoter	22,870
Market analyst	32,000
Retail supervisor	41,200

Sources: New York State Department of Labor; U.S. Bureau of Labor Statistics; WetFeet research

Resources

Association for Retailers Online (www.shop.org)

Center for Retailing Education and Research (www.cba.ufl.edu/CRER)

National Retail Federation (www.nrf.com)

Key NYC Retail Companies

Company	2006 Revenue ($M)	1-Yr. Change (%)	Employees	Website
Toys R Us*	11,100	–4.0	157,000	www7.toysrus.com
Great Atlantic & Pacific Tea	8,740	–19.5	38,000	www.aptea.com
IAC/InterActiveCorp*	5,754	–7.1	28,000	www.iac.com
Foot Locker	5,653	5.6	44,109	www.footlocker-inc.com
Asbury Automotive Group*	5,541	4.5	8,800	www.asburyauto.com
Barnes & Noble	5,103	4.7	39,000	www.barnesandnobleinc.com
Macy's East**	4,428	–11.7	29,100	www.macys.com
Saks Fifth Avenue Enterprises*	2,737	12.4	15,000	www.saksfifthavenue.com
Bloomingdale's**	2,058	17.8	11,300	www.bloomingdales.com
Duane Reade**	1,600	15.6	6,300	www.duanereade.com
Aéropostale	1,204	24.9	9,621	www.aeropostale.com
Columbia House Co.***	1,000	–16.7	2,200	www.columbiahouse.com
Finlay Enterprises	990	7.2	6,000	www.finlayenterprises.com
Paxar*	809	0.6	9,700	www.paxar.com
J. Crew Group*	804	16.6	8,200	www.jcrew.com
Henry Modell & Co.***	500	7.5	3,500	www.modells.com
Barneys New York**	410	6.8	1,400	www.barneys.com
Hanover Direct*	403	–2.8	2,200	www.hanoverdirect.com
Loehmann's Holdings**	365	4.5	1,784	www.loehmanns.com
Cache, Inc.*	266	7.7	2,700	www.cache.com
Alloy	195	–51.5	2,723	www.alloy.com

*2005 figures
**2004 figures
***2003 figures (most recent available)
Sources: *Crain's New York Business Book of Lists*; Hoover's; WetFeet analysis

TECHNOLOGY

New York's technology and new media sector is a $9.2 billion industry, according to the New York City Economic Development Corporation, with some 4,000 high-tech and new media companies. No longer contained to Silicon Alley south of 41st Street, these companies have now spread through Upper Manhattan, Brooklyn, Queens, and Staten Island. For the most part, NYC hosts specialty software companies rather than powerhouses that require sprawling corporate campuses. The exception is Microsoft, which is increasing its presence in New York to be closer to its many clients here.

Businesses and individual consumers are the main purchasers of computer software, which is sold through both retail and business-to-business channels. In either case, companies that sell computer software are intensely focused on the needs and desires of customers. The quickest way to talk yourself out of a job in this segment is to make the technology seem more important than the end user.

The Internet has meant a sea change in the software industry. Many software users now download their purchases from providers' websites, forgoing CDs and packaging and getting straight to business. And the subscription ASP (application service provider) model, in which users access software and databases that are stored on the vendors' servers via the Web, is proving attractive in areas from gaming to business software.

Job Prospects

One of New York City's strongest job growth areas in 2005 was in computer technology. In addition to talented software developers, project managers who can relate the technical issues to the marketing and business folks are also in demand. Marketing is critical to the success of any computer software product, partly because there are so many companies competing in the software market and partly because computers are still new to a lot of people. In fact, in most companies that produce computer software, the marketing department calls the shots.

For those with strong communication skills, technical writers are employed at most computer software companies to write user documentation, either for publication in the form of manuals or, increasingly, as online help. The industry also employs—in descending order of technical expertise—software testers, customer service reps, sales personnel, and staff for the usual variety of business functions, from HR to accounting to marketing.

Key Technology Jobs

Key Job	Average NYC Salary ($)	Entry Level ($)
Vice president product development	150,000	85,000
Enterprise architect	125,340	85,450
Application architect	108,200	77,250
Project manager	99,500	75,000
Software engineer, applications	84,490	60,360
Software engineer, system software	86,870	56,220
Help desk specialist	48,000	36,000
Technical writer	64,520	44,850
Hardware engineer	82,530	60,880
Systems engineer	160,000	140,000
Quality analyst/tester	70,250	551,500

Sources: New York State Department of Labor; WetFeet research

Resources

The Industry Standard (www.thestandard.com)

New York Software Industry Association (www.nysia.org)

Red Herring (www.redherring.com)

Software Information & Industry Association (www.siia.net)

Key NYC Technology Companies

Firm	2005 Revenue ($M)	1-Yr. Change (%)	Employees	Website
IBM	91,134	–5.4	329,373	www.ibm.com
ITT Industries	7,427	9.8	44,000	www.ittind.com
CA	3,530	7.8	15,300	www.ca.com
Symbol Technologies	1,766	1.9	5,400	www.symbol.com
Moody's	1,732	20.4	2,900	www.moodys.com
Dun & Bradstreet	1,444	2.1	4,350	www.dnb.com
Take-Two Interactive Software	1,203	6.6	2,002	www.take2games.com
The BISYS Group	1,063	2.5	5,300	www.bisys.com
Cognizant Technology Solutions	886	51.0	24,300	www.cognizant.com
NASDAQ	880	62.8	917	www.nasdaq.com
Paxar	809	0.6	9,700	www.paxar.com
Scientific Games	782	7.7	3,550	www.scientificgames.com
Aeroflex	463	11.9	2,640	www.aeroflex.com
Investment Technology Group	408	22.0	714	www.itginc.com
Information Builders	300	n/a	1,750	www.informationbuilders.com
Verint Systems	250	29.6	1,200	www.verintsystems.com
Atari**	219	–44.7	492	www.atari.com
eSpeed	146	–12.4	400	www.espeed.com
24/7 Real Media	140	63.9	368	www.247realmedia.com
Register.com*	101	–3.3	511	www.register.com

*2004 figures

**2006 figures

Sources: *Crain's New York Business Book of Lists*; Hoover's; WetFeet analysis

TELECOMMUNICATIONS

Telecommunications is a mammoth industry, comprising companies that make hardware, produce software, and provide services. Hardware includes a vast range of products that enable communication across the entire planet, from video broadcasting satellites to telephone handsets to fiber-optic transmission cables. Services include running the switches that control the phone system, making access to the Internet available, and configuring private networks by which international corporations conduct business. Software makes it all work, from sending and receiving email to relaying satellite data to controlling telephone switching equipment.

The wireless sector should continue to grow in 2005. A Deloitte research report predicts there will be nearly two billion wireless subscribers worldwide by the end of 2005. Technologies will continue to converge in your cell phone, with cameras, music players, email, video, and even TV, all available now.

Meanwhile, broadband continues to penetrate markets and is expected to outnumber dial-up connections in many countries, bringing a range of new broadband appliances to market, including home security devices and videophones.

Job Prospects

While employment in the industry is expected to grow, it won't be at breakneck speed. According to the BLS, telecom employment is expected to grow by 7 percent between 2002 and 2012, slower than the 16 percent average growth for all industries combined. Debt and excess transmission capacity will be drags on the bigger companies' growth.

In this field, demand for workers will vary depending on which side of the technology you're on. For example, as new voice recognition technology improves productivity, jobs like telephone and directory assistance operators will continue to decrease in number. But the need for engineers who develop that technology will increase.

The outlook is good in telecom sectors that are bringing exciting *new* technologies to market. High-speed data services, voice communications over the Internet, and wireless networking will be hiring, and small companies are good places to find these jobs. Electrical and electronics engineers, computer software engineers, systems analysts, and customer service professionals can all find opportunities here. Line installers and repairers should also find work as businesses seek to increase connections to suppliers and customers, and residential customers add broadband service.

Key Telecommunications Jobs

Key Jobs	Average NYC Salary ($)
Customer service director	114,600
Network operations manager	90,200
Network planning manager	85,100
Product manager	67,200
Service delivery manager	80,900
Marketing director	130,400
Radio frequency applications engineering manager	122,200

Sources: WetFeet research

Resources

Telecommunications Industry Association (www.tiaonline.org)

Telecommunications Magazine (www.telecoms-mag.com)

Key NYC Telecommunications Firms

Firm	2005 Revenue ($M)	1-Yr. Change (%)	Employees	Website
Siemens	90,670	–3.0	461,000	www.usa.siemens.com
Verizon Communications	75,112	5.4	250,000	www.verizon.com
L-3 Communications	9,445	36.9	59,500	www.l-3com.com
Lucent	9,441	4.4	30,500	www.lucent.com
Cablevision Systems	5,176	4.9	20,425	www.cablevision.com
Avaya	4,902	20.5	19,100	www.avaya.com
NTL	3,351	163.2	13,650	www.ntl.com
IDT	2,469	11.3	5,397	www.idt.net
Insight Communications	1,003	11.1	3,625	www.insight-com.com
Comverse Technology	959	25.3	5,050	www.cmvt.com
Comtech Telecommunications	308	37.8	1,090	www.comtechtel.com
Verint	250	29.6	1,200	www.verintsystems.com
Loral Space & Communications	197	–62.2	2,600	www.loral.com
Loren Communications Intl.	125	n/a	500	www.lorencommunications.com
Globecomm Systems	110	25.7	155	www.globecommsystems.com
Globix	95.7	56.4	330	www.globix.com
Lynch Interactive*	87.8	0.3	356	www.lynchinteractivecorp.com
Net2Phone	78.8	–4.8	287	www.net2phone.com
E.A. Technologies	47.1	n/a	20	n/a
Porta Systems**	19.6	–8.5	274	www.portasystems.com

*2004 figures
**2003 figures
Sources: *Crain's New York Business Book of Lists 2006*; Hoover's; WetFeet analysis

Major Careers

Opportunities for professionals in certain occupations such as accounting, information technology, human resources, sales, marketing, and public relations are available broadly across a number of industries. Although companies now value more and more specialized industry knowledge, there exists a foundation of training and skills that is the same regardless of the industry in which they are applied. According to a pharmaceutical company employment representative, "What people may not understand is that you don't have to be a scientist to work here. There's great demand in our industry for talented people with backgrounds in marketing, sales, and other nonscientific areas."

ACCOUNTING

Accounting concerns itself with the day-to-day operations of bookkeeping. Accountants balance the books, track expenses and revenue, execute payroll, and pay the bills. They also compile all of the financial data needed to issue a company's financial statements in accordance with government regulations. When most people think of accounting, they imagine a public accountant who has passed an exam to become a state-licensed certified public accountant (CPA). Public accountants work at independent public accounting firms, file a client's taxes, and audit a client's financial information.

But accountants are taking a step away from the ledger sheets and are becoming essential to every successful business team. They're the ones who understand the language of money and a company's complex financial situation. Consequently, accountants are increasingly being called on to offer advice and even make business decisions based on hard facts rather than on speculation or gut instinct.

Accounting jobs require critical, detail-oriented thinking. If you have a knack for using numbers to understand patterns that influence business, you're going to be valuable to a company. If you can't crunch and analyze, this isn't going to be the right job for you. You should also like—and be good at—solving problems: thinking critically about the numbers with which you're working.

Companies large and small generally have their own staff accountants to advise management and to perform internal audits and day-to-day bookkeeping. In addition to the private sector, government entities such as city, county, state, and federal bureaucracies also employ a large number of accountants.

Job Prospects

The accounting profession is growing faster than the average because of both business growth and the increased scrutiny on corporate finances. The Sarbanes-Oxley Act requires companies to tighten their accounting practices and has consequently increased demand. The BLS projects New York employers will need 1,520 new accountants every year until 2012. So, despite all the recent accounting scandals, now is not a bad time to be looking for an entry-level job in accounting. Clients need accountants in bad times as well as good, and Big Four firms always need bodies to do the lower-level scut work; in return, employees get a wealth of exposure to accounting issues, as well as a Big Four name on their resumes, which will help them in a variety of business careers.

Far and away, the most positions available in public accounting are in audit, with tax coming in second. The need for forensic accountants—specialized accountants who focus on digging into clients' balance sheets to look for red flags—is growing as the industry and its clients look to rebuild their reputations. Demand for in-house accounting employees is expected to be strongest in the health-care and manufacturing industries, though companies in every industry will always need accountants to handle their financial matters.

Key Accounting Positions

Key Jobs	Median NYC Salary ($)
Accountant or auditor	66,140
Audit manager	113,986
Bookkeeping clerk	35,790
Budget analyst	63,300
Cost accountant	50,665
Payroll clerk	37,300
Tax examiner	68,430
Tax preparer	47,750
Treasurer	197,257

Sources: New York State Department of Labor; WetFeet research

Resources

AccountingWEB (www.accountingweb.com)

American Institute of Certified Public Accountants (www.aicpa.org)

Careers in Accounting (WetFeet Insider Guide available from www.wetfeet.com)

CPA Exam (www.cpa-exam.org)

Institute of Internal Auditors (www.theiia.org)

Institute of Management Accountants (www.imanet.org)

International Federation of Accountants (www.ifac.org)

New York State Society of CPAs (www.nysscpa.org)

DESIGN

Designers work on everything from airplane chairs to the patterns on fabric, and have a hand in virtually every industry, from textiles (clothing design) to publishing (graphic design). Even your groceries are designed: Take a look at the cans and packages on your local supermarket's shelves. From the package shapes to the printing on them, all are products of a designer.

Design encompasses a wide range of fields. Interior designers concern themselves with the spaces inside buildings. Fashion designers determine the look and function of our clothes. Graphic designers convey ideas through type and image. The ubiquitous logo for Coca-Cola, for instance, is the work of a graphic designer, while Levi's 501 jeans are the work of a fashion designer.

Designers often specialize. For instance, industrial designers—those who focus on the design of objects and machines—might specialize in kitchen equipment such as the shape and function of food processors, electric can openers, and blenders.

Job Prospects

The BLS expects the number of design jobs to rise at a rate greater than the average for all jobs between 2000 and 2010. Job growth will be especially strong in areas such as graphic design and industrial design. There's an increasing need for interior designers as well. And talented video game designers will find themselves in great demand moving forward; right now, demand for these folks peaks with the release of new versions of gaming platforms, but as gaming moves onto the Web, expect demand to be steadier.

But competition for jobs is still fierce, as design is a very popular field; employers will be looking for only the most talented people. Illustrators are suffering in the current market; many of those who would have hired illustrators in the past now prefer to use increasingly available stock images rather than pay artists to render original sketches. However, illustrators and other artists may find an outlet for their talents in electronic art or animation.

Key Design Positions

Key Jobs	Median NYC Salary ($)
Advertising graphic designer	53,490
Illustrator	52,600
Industrial designer	48,210
Interior designer	53,300
Technical illustrator	55,341
Web art director	115,932
Web designer	46,000

Sources: WetFeet research

Resources

American Institute of Graphic Arts (www.aiga.org)

Art Directors Club (www.adcglobal.org)

Communication Arts (www.commarts.com)

Graphic Artists Guild (www.gag.org)

Graphic Arts Information Network (www.gain.org)

Industrial Designers Society of America (www.idsa.org)

International Interior Design Association (www.iida.org)

Society of Publication Designers (www.spd.org)

HUMAN RESOURCES

The role of human resources (HR) in business has evolved from an exclusively in-house function to become its own industry providing a complete range of HR services. There is a growing need for HR professionals who have a strong grounding in business, organizational development, accounting, statistics, and legal issues. Many in the field have master's degrees and certifications. Top HR officers in corporations are often key members of the executive team, sitting alongside their counterparts in research, finance, operations, sales, and marketing.

While job requirements may vary from one type of business to another, HR generalists are responsible for attracting and retaining employees, arranging and overseeing training, designing compensation plans, selecting and managing benefit programs, and advising management on employment law. Other HR roles include recruiters, trainers, outplacement specialists, and HR specialists, who provide advice on compensation, benefit administration, and HR information systems.

Job Prospects

The outlook for HR jobs is about the same as those for the economy overall. The BLS projects that 27,788 new human resources jobs will be created between 2000 and 2010, an increase of 12.7 percent.

Some sectors will likely see greater growth and, with it, a greater demand for HR professionals. Computer and data processing services represent the area of fastest growth; the BLS expects HR jobs in the computer industry to grow by 66 percent. Opportunities in residential care and home health care are also expected to grow rapidly: The BLS considers these the second-best growth areas for HR. This reflects a general truism within HR: Changes in lifestyle and population trends are reflected in HR opportunities.

One such example, related to the aging U.S. population, is the need for more HR workers in hospitals and in allied health services. Hospitals ranked eighth in overall projected HR employment for 2010, and allied health ranked eighth in percentage change from 2000 to 2010.

Key Human Resources Positions

Key Jobs	Median NYC Salary ($)
Compensation and benefits analyst	57,620
Human resources employment specialist	47,800
Human resources manager	91,190
Training and development specialist	58,840

Sources: New York State Department of Labor; WetFeet research

Resources

Careers in Human Resources (WetFeet Insider Guide available from www.wetfeet.com)

Electronic Recruiting Exchange (www.erexchange.com)

Employee Benefit Research Institute (www.ebri.org)

HR.com

HR Magazine (www.shrm.org/hrmagazine)

Human Resources Association of New York (www.hrny.org)

Society for Human Resource Management (www.shrm.org)

Staffing Industry Analysts (www.sireview.com)

Workforce Management (www.workforce.com)

INFORMATION TECHNOLOGY

Email, personal computers, and the Internet: These products of the information age have become common currency among working professionals. They make your life simpler by enabling faster communication, providing tools for more effective work, and giving you access to vast information with the click of a mouse. But they also introduce a risk factor that isn't totally within your control: If your computer fails or the network connection goes down, you lose time and often money.

The range of IT jobs is vast. The skills needed to set up an office network—install the cables, configure the computers, and keep them running—are quite different from those required to set up and customize an automated-payroll software system. A database specialist needs still other skills to administer the ever-changing complex of information generated by enterprise software applications and the company website, including files on visitors who have signed on as members or purchased something. Each of these jobs requires different skills and in-depth technical knowledge. As a result, many IT jobs are highly specialized, focusing on a small aspect within the grand design of a company's network.

INSIDER TIP

A New York recruiting firm that specializes in IT placement reported in September 2005 that 75 percent of the positions it fills are for the financial services sector.

But no matter what job they do, all IT professionals focus on improving the usability and efficiency of technological systems and processes. Their goal is a smoothly functioning computer network—free of bugs, glitches, and interruptions—that provides an effective flow of information so the company can keep improving its work processes, customer retention and acquisition, and other aspects of its business.

Job Prospects

IT employment is higher today than it was at the peak of the dotcom bubble. While outsourcing has long been considered a job seeker's bane, a new study from the Association for Computing Machinery says that only 2 to 3 percent of IT jobs will go to lower-wage countries such as India and China over the coming decade. The upside is that this migration makes way for upgraded IT opportunities in the United States—the higher-value work of applying information technology to other fields, like biology and business.

In New York City, the number of IT job openings is up 11 percent from 2005 to 11,000 in February 2006. A report from CityEconomist shows the highest demand is for programmers who speak Java, Unix, SQL, and HTML. SAP programmers? Not so much.

"The industry is becoming more consolidated," a seasoned insider says. "People who don't want to be in this industry have left. In some ways, it's a nicer place to be. People aren't in it for the money the way they used to be."

Key Information Technology Positions

Key Jobs	Median NYC Salary ($)
Application architect	77,250
Chief information officer	114,750
Database administrator	79,760
Database manager	82,750
IT manager	81,500
Project manager	75,000
Quality assurance/tester	51,500
Software developer	74,660
Systems analyst	78,290
Web developer	53,250

Sources: WetFeet research

Resources

Careers in Information Technology
(WetFeet Insider Guide available from www.wetfeet.com)

The Industry Standard (www.thestandard.com)

Red Herring (www.redherring.com)

Software and Information Industry Association (www.siia.net)

Wired magazine (www.wired.com)

SALES AND MARKETING

A salesperson must become an expert in his field—be it telecommunications equipment, retail, real estate, or pharmaceuticals—supplying answers and information as much as goods or services. The contemporary salesperson is more a listener than a talker, and she tailors the sale to fit the customer's needs.

These days, to ensure client satisfaction, salespeople are often expected to handle paperwork, address client problems and grievances, and manage special circumstances (for example, supervising unusual delivery conditions or alternative payment plans).

Wages vary greatly. Base pay may be literally $0.00 per year for those confident enough to take a commission-only position. But salaries fall all along the income spectrum, and earnings at the high end can be in the six-figure range. Most sales positions offer a small base salary and pay a commission on each deal. Management positions generally command a reasonable base salary and don't earn commissions because managers usually aren't directly responsible for sales.

Marketing, on the other hand, is the intermediary function between product development and sales. Marketers create, manage, and enhance brands. (A brand can be thought of as the way consumers perceive a particular company or its products and how a company reinforces or enhances those perceptions through its overall communications—its logo, advertising, packaging, and so on.)

In the consumer products industry, marketing (called brand management) is the lead function. In other industries marketing may play a supporting role to another function. At a high-tech company, for instance, marketing may play a supporting role to research and development. And in advertising, market research and public relations (a specialized marketing function) *are* the industry.

Job Prospects

The BLS says sales jobs will increase faster than average over the next ten years because of global competition. Sales opportunities vary by industry sector. The technology industry pays the most and employs the most. Next are finance, insurance, architecture, and engineering. There is less demand in computers, wholesale electronics, auto dealership, and machinery and equipment wholesaling.

In New York, sales ranks as number 21 out of the 25 most wanted positions through 2012 with 1,320 jobs to fill annually. Insurance agents and real estate agents can expect slower-than-average employment growth. Retail opportunities are expected to grow faster. Customer service jobs are in even higher demand with 1,410 positions to fill each year.

Key Sales and Marketing Positions

Key Jobs	Median NYC Salary ($)
Market research analyst	59,800
Marketing manager	132,310
Promotions manager	118,310
Public relations manager	104,880
Sales manager	142,940
Wholesale sales representative	57,880

Sources: New York State Department of Labor; WetFeet research

Resources

American Marketing Association (www.marketingpower.com)

Business Marketing Association (www.marketing.org)

Careers in Marketing & Market Research (WetFeet Insider Guide available from www.wetfeet.com)

Justsell.com

MarketingSherpa (www.marketingsherpa.com)

New York American Marketing Association (www.nyama.org)

Employer Rankings

New York City's Largest Employers, 2006

Rank	Employer	NYC Employees	Total Employees
1	NewYork-Presbyterian Healthcare System	29,921	55,407
2	Citigroup	27,144	307,000
3	JPMorgan Chase	20,257	168,847
4	Verizon Communications	18,500	250,000
5	Continuum Health Partners	16,108	16,108
6	Federated Department Stores	14,000	232,000
7	New York University	13,494	13,494
8	Columbia University	12,707	13,343
9	North Shore–Long Island Jewish Health System	12,683	28,518
10	Time Warner	12,500	87,850
11	Mount Sinai Hospital	11,629	11,629
12	Saint Vincent Catholic Medical Centers	11,511	11,948
13	Consolidated Edison	11,423	14,537
14	Montefiore Medical Center	10,311	10,933
15	Morgan Stanley	9,900	53,218
16	PersonalTouch Home Care	10,100	16,300
17	The Bank of New York Company	8,800	22,901
18	UPS	8,750	407,000
19	Viacom	8,238	31,429
20	Memorial Sloan-Kettering Cancer Center	8,251	8,574
21	The Goldman Sachs Group	8,006	20,722
22	Merrill Lynch	7,750	50,600
23	Pfizer	7,106	112,385
24	American International Group	6,169	97,000
25	NYU Medical Center	5,086	5,086

Sources: *Crain's New York Business Book of Lists 2006*; Hoover's

NYC Employers Among the "100 Most Desirable MBA Employers"

Rank	Company	Industry
1	McKinsey	Consulting
2	Goldman Sachs Group	Investment banking
6	Citigroup	Financial services
10	Morgan Stanley	Investment banking
13	Lehman Brothers	Investment banking
17	Deloitte	Accounting, consulting
20	Merrill Lynch	Financial services
28	UBS	Financial services
30	PepsiCo	Manufacturing
33	American Express	Financial services
38	JPMorgan Chase	Financial services
41	Deutsche Bank	Financial services
42	L'Oréal	Manufacturing
43	Accenture	Consulting
47	Pfizer	Pharmaceutical manufacturing
50	PricewaterhouseCoopers	Accounting
67	Ernst & Young	Accounting
82	KPMG	Accounting
80	Colgate-Palmolive	Manufacturing
88	Saks	Retail

Sources: Ranking based on Universum Communications poll, 2006; WetFeet research

Help Wanted?

Job Postings

Recruiters

Job Fairs

Employment and Temp Agencies

Networking

“ ” I just think that you need to do everything and anything in a job search that’s legal.

You’re new in town. You need a job. How do you get past that I’m-not-in-Kansas-anymore mixture of excitement and fear, and get down to work? A job search in New York City can be intimidating, even for natives. Prime positions are filled quickly, and competition is fierce. To make this monster goal more manageable, break it down into simple steps.

In the last chapter you gathered information about potential employers and the jobs they need to fill. The next step is to target your search and identify what positions are available and where.

Job Postings

Gone are the days of sitting in the coffee shop circling promising want ads with a pen. The Internet has made it easier than ever to learn what jobs are available, assess the culture and benefits of a potential employer, plus read the latest annual report, check discussion boards to see what other job seekers have to say, search for representative salary ranges, and submit your resume—all without getting out of your pajamas.

Job postings can be found on company websites, general classified advertising (either online or in print), industry and association publications and websites, and the career offices of colleges and universities.

COMPANY WEBSITES

Most large companies maintain sophisticated websites with a wealth of information for job seekers. Under the career section you can often find job openings, descriptions of how the company is organized, and sometimes profiles of employees who hold representative positions. But don’t stop there. You can learn valuable information by reviewing the investor relations, press information, and company history sections.

Employers often use online application systems to solicit resumes. These systems are usually easy and convenient to use, but don't rely on them exclusively to get your resume noticed. Unless you've included the perfect keywords to match a hiring manager's search elements, your set of perfect qualifications will be just one of an electronic crowd.

Use company websites to look for available jobs, but also for clues to the corporate culture:

- Is it for-profit or nonprofit?
- What is the company's size, number of employees, annual revenue, or growth rate?
- What is the pace of work? Dynamic and always changing? Or more routine?
- Does the company support family-friendly policies and benefits?
- What opportunities exist for women? How many women are represented in upper management?
- Is the company environmentally conscious?
- Are people who work at the company in it for the money? Or are they more interested in quality—to offer the best product or service in their industry?
- What kind of recognition or awards has the company received?

BE A NAME-DROPPER

Once you identify a job opening, don't rely exclusively on submitting your resume in response, whether by mail, email, or an online application. Literally hundreds of people are applying for the same position, and it's easy for your perfect qualifications to be overlooked. A better strategy is to find someone you know who works in the organization and ask whether you can use his or her name in your cover letter. Better yet, ask for a referral or personal introduction to the appropriate hiring manager.

CLASSIFIED ADS

The want ads still exist, of course, but most papers—notably the *Wall Street Journal* and the *New York Times*—now sponsor online ads. In addition, a number of Internet job boards like Monster.com encourage you to post your resume as well as search jobs in the profession, industry, and geographic region of your choice. For every job listed, piles of resumes are submitted. For certain jobs, your chances might be better if you use a smaller, local NYC job board because an employer seeking a local hire (without relocation issues) may want to limit responses to a manageable number.

DON'T FALL INTO THE INTERNET BLACK HOLE

It's easy to get distracted while online. You start out on the Merrill Lynch site where a press release about community service work catches your eye. Before you know it, you're reading about how to become a teaching fellow in New York Public Schools because your brother-in-law might be interested. One thing leads to the next and soon you're at movies.com checking out the schedule for the Film Forum.

To stay on target, set limits for the amount of time you'll stay online, and ask yourself before you start: What are my goals for this session?

General Job Posting Websites

CareerBuilder (www.careerbuilder.com)

CareerMole (www.careermole.com)

Executive Staffers (www.executivestaffers.com)

Monster (www.monster.com)

NowHiring.com (www.nowhiring.com)

Wall Street Journal's Career Journal (www.careerjournal.com)

Yahoo! HotJobs (www.hotjobs.com)

New York City Job Posting Websites

Craigslist (newyork.craigslist.org)

New York City Economic Development Corp. (www.newyorkbiz.com)

New York Times Job Market (www.nytimes.com/pages/jobs)

NYC.gov (To see open city government positions, select "Government" from the top navigation bar and then select "Working for NYC" from the left menu.)

NYCareers.com

Workforce1 (www.ci.nyc.ny.us/html/wia/home.html)

INSIDER TIP

Companies often post vacancies on their corporate website before listing on job boards or classifieds elsewhere. Get a jump on the competition by checking the websites of your targeted list of companies.

Industry- and Career-Specific Job Posting Websites

Accounting

Accountemps (www.accountemps.com)
CareerBank.com
CPA Career Center (www.cpa2biz.com/career/default.htm)
Jobs in the Money (www.jobsinthemoney.com/accounting-jobs.cfm)

Advertising

Advertising Media Internet Company (www.amic.com)
Advertising Research Foundation (www.arfsite.org)
Association of National Advertisers (www.ana.net/hr/hr.htm)
Talent Zoo (www.talentzoo.com)

Construction

AEC WorkForce (www.aecworkforce.com)
ConstructionJobs.com
National Society of Professional Engineers (www.nspe.org)

Consider a post-graduate internship in fields where entry is especially competitive, like publishing and the arts. "So many of my friends are totally embarrassed about getting internships after college, but a post-grad internship is such a good idea," says one insider. "It pays to make contacts and get practical experience for your resume. If you're really practical and say, 'I have to get a real job,' you have a hard road ahead of you."

Design

24 Seven Talent (www.24seventalent.com)
Coroflot (www.coroflot.com)
Creative Hotlist (www.creativehotlist.com)

Education

Education Week (www.agentk-12.org)
HigherEdJobs.com
New York City Department of Education (www.nycenet.edu/teachnyc)
New York State Department of Education (www.deptofed.org)

Entertainment and Sports

Casting Call (web.actorsequity.org/CastingSearch/)
EntertainmentCareers.net New York Job Listings (www.entertainmentcareers.net/sbjobs/ny.asp)
New York State Broadcasters Association Job Bank (www.nysbroadcastersassn.org; open "Job Bank" link on left)
Playbill Job Listing (www.playbill.com/jobs/find)
Variety Careers (www.variety.com/index.asp?layout=variety_careers)
Work In Sports (www.workinsports.com)

Beware of outdated postings. Small nonprofits, in particular, can be slow to update their sites. You spend hours crafting your cover letter for your perfect job only to learn it was filled months ago.

Fashion

24 Seven Talent (www.24seventalent.com)
Fashion Career Center (www.fashioncareercenter.com)
Fashion Net (www.fashion.net/jobs)
Fashion Windows (www.fashionwindows.com)
Style Careers (www.stylecareers.com)

Finance and Insurance

American Academy of Actuaries (www.contingencies.org)
American Bankers Association (aba.careerbank.com)
BankJobs.com
CareerBank.com
GreatInsuranceJobs.com
Jobs in the Money (www.jobsinthemoney.com)

Health Care

CampusRN.com
Comprehensive Health Care Staffing (www.comphealth.com)
HEALTHeCAREERS Network (www.healthecareers.com)
JobScience.com
MedCAREERS (www.medcareers.com)
MedHunters.com
MedJump.com
Medployment.com
Medzilla.com

Hospitality and Food Service

Hcareers.com
Hospitality Jobs Online (www.hospitalityonline.com)
New York State Hospitality & Tourism Association Job Bank (www.sma.new-jobs.com/ny)
WineandHospitalityJobs.com

Human Resources

Electronic Recruiting Exchange's Job Board (www.erexchange.com/jobboard)
HR Hub (www.hrhub.com)
I Hire HR (www.ihirehr.com)
Jobs4HR.com
My HR Jobs (www.myhrjobs.com)

Legal

EmpLawyerNet (www.emplawyernet.com; paid subscription required)
FindLaw Career Center (careers.findlaw.com)
Law Info Career Center (jobs.lawinfo.com)
Lawjobs.com
Legalstaff.com

Manufacturing

ASME (American Society of Mechanical Engineers) Career Center (www.asme.org/jobs)
ChemicalEngineer.com
ChemJobs.net
DNAjobs.com

INSIDER TIP

Look at resumes other job seekers have posted online. How do your qualifications compare with those of others? How does your competition present itself? What can you learn that will be useful in your own search?

Publishing

Copy Editor Job Board (www.copyeditor.com)
Editor & Publisher Classifieds (www.editorandpublisher.com)
JournalismJobs.com
Magazine Publishers of America Job Bank (jobs.magazine.org)
Media Bistro (www.mediabistro.com)
Publishers Marketplace (www.publishersmarketplace.com0

Real Estate

RealEstateJobs.com
Real-Jobs.com

Retail

AllRetailJobs.com
Hcareers.com (www.retailjobs.hcareers.com)
iHireRetail.com
Retailology.com
Style Careers (www.stylecareers.com)

WATCH OUT!

Just as you can learn a great deal about a company online, so can they learn about you. You might want to think twice about that racy blog post or a wild party report on MySpace. You never know exactly who's looking. Companies can and will check you out before they make you an offer.

Sales and Marketing

American Marketing Association's Career Center (www.marketingpower.com/content966.php)
Jobs4Sales.com
SalesHeads.com
SalesJobs.com

Technology/Information Technology

ComputerJobs.com (www.newyork.computerjobs.com)
Dice (www.dice.com)
Eric Robert Staffing Solutions (www.ericrobert.com)
JobsNetWORK (http://jobsnetwork.siia.net)
JustTechJobs.com
ComputerWork.com (http://newyork.computerwork.com)
Techies.com

Telecommunications

ActiveWireless.com
JustWirelessJobs.com
Telecomcareers.net
TelecomEngineer.com
Thingamajob.com (http://telecommunications.thingamajob.com)

INSIDER TIP

Searching job postings can result in more than a list of job openings. You can also:

- **Discover industry keywords to use in your resume.**
- **Assess the demand for your skills in a particular industry or geographic area.**

INDUSTRY OR PROFESSIONAL PUBLICATIONS

Often you can successfully hone your search by targeting newsletters and job boards sponsored by professional associations or other industry-specific sources. These tend to be viewed by a smaller audience, decreasing the competition for posted openings. You'll want to conduct some research to find a list of publications for your particular career or industry. See the "Resources" sections of the industry and career profiles in the previous chapter for examples of industry publications.

Career Resource Centers

If you're a college student, take advantage of your campus career center. Not only do recruiters of major employers regularly visit certain colleges and universities, but you can also learn about alumni who work for the employers on your interest list.

The Mid-Manhattan branch of the New York Public Library hosts a well-stocked career resource center and offers classes and support groups:

Job Information Center
Mid-Manhattan Library, 2nd floor
455 Fifth Avenue at 40th Street
New York, NY 10016
212-340-0836
mmjobinf@nypl.org

The City of New York also has five Workforce1 Career Centers, which offer employment-related services and resources to job seekers:

Brooklyn:
9 Bond Street, 5th Floor
Brooklyn, NY 11201
Telephone: 718-246-5219
Open Monday through Friday: 9:00 a.m. to 5:00 p.m.

Bronx:
358 East 149th Street, 2nd Floor
Bronx, NY 10455
Telephone: 718-960-7099
Monday, Tuesday, Thursday, and Friday: 8:30 a.m. to 5:00 p.m.
Wednesday: 8:30 a.m. to 8:00 p.m.

Bronx - CUNY on the Concourse:
2501 Grand Concourse, 3rd Floor
Bronx, NY 10468
Telephone: 718-960-6900
Open Monday through Saturday: 9:00 a.m. to 5:00 p.m.

Lower Manhattan Affiliate:
220 Church Street, 3rd Floor
New York, NY 10013
Telephone: 212-442-1355
Open Monday through Friday: 9:00 a.m. to 5:00 p.m.

Upper Manhattan:
215 West 125th Street, 6th Floor
New York, NY 10027
Telephone: 917-493-7000
Open Monday, Wednesday, and Friday: 8:30 a.m. to 5:00 p.m.
Tuesday and Thursday: 8:30 a.m to 9:00 p.m.

Queens:
168-46 91st Avenue, 2nd Floor
Jamaica, NY 11432
Telephone: 718-557- 6755
Open Monday through Friday: 8:30 a.m. to 6:00 p.m.

Recruiters

The mere mention of the word *recruiters* makes some job seekers run screaming. Sometimes called *headhunters*, they can be slick and hard-selling, and they'll drop you in a flash in favor of a more qualified candidate. But they can also get you exactly the kind of access to a hiring manager that you want. "They think they know everything," says one New York job seeker. "Their interviewing styles are very abrasive—always on the attack versus inquiring about transferable skills. I would prefer to struggle on my own than listen to someone barking things at me. Just personal preference."

If you find you're not getting interviews based on your own efforts or that you need to expand your contacts beyond your current network, consider using the services of a professional recruiter. If you're searching at the executive level where jobs may not be publicly posted, a recruiter can be even more helpful.

Recruiters come in a variety of flavors:

- **Corporate recruiters** are the HR folks who are employed by a company to find and qualify new employees for the organization. For the purposes of this discussion, however, we use "recruiters" to refer to third-party recruiters.
- **Third-party recruiters** are subcontracted to and paid for by a company. They work in one of two ways:
    - **Retained recruiters** have an exclusive contract with the company and are primarily used for executive-level positions.
    - **Contingency recruiters** are paid a fee only if the company hires a candidate discovered through their efforts.

If you find yourself on the phone with a recruiter who says she has the perfect job for you, keep in mind that she gets her paycheck from the hiring employer. Third-party recruiters generally receive 20 to 30 percent of a placed candidate's first-year salary. The recruiter may do a fine job presenting your skills and helping you negotiate the best deal possible, but understand that her primary allegiance is not to you.

HOW RECRUITERS WORK

Recruiting firms are employment agencies. Companies hire executive recruiters to find and bring in candidates for management positions—anyone with two years of professional work experience on up. The corporation is the recruiter's client, and the job candidate is the product. Thus, recruiters normally find a person for the job, not a job for the person. This is an important distinction.

Most firms specialize in some manner, either regionally, by profession (accounting, legal, advertising, marketing, for example), or industry—such as high-tech or pharmaceutical. Some firms have exclusive contracts to do all of a company's outsource hiring.

FINDING A RECRUITER

Step one is finding a recruiting firm that works in your field. Begin by asking people you know. If your dream job is at a specific company, find out who does their recruiting. If you belong to a professional association, ask your colleagues for names of recruiters who specialize in your industry. You can find contact information for recruiters online, but it's best to ask for references from those who have worked with them.

GRILLING YOUR RECRUITER

Here are some questions to ask if you are contacted by a recruiter and asked to send your resume:

Is there a specific job you have in mind for me?
Once you receive my resume, when can I expect to hear from you again?
Will you get my consent before sending my resume to one of your clients?

Once you've found a firm, choose an individual recruiter with whom you can develop a good relationship. "Above all, find a person you trust," says Howard Hegwer, a managing partner of Management Recruiters International, in Seattle. "If there is not a bond of trust, then the relationship will be unproductive and disappointing."

Put the recruiter to the test. How established is the firm? How long has the person been recruiting? What did he or she do before? Does he or she have a solid working knowledge of your field? Years of recruiting experience are great, but not absolutely essential. Someone who spent 20 years in consulting can probably step right in and act as an excellent recruiter for consulting jobs.

Be certain you understand how the recruiting process will work. If you are currently employed—and hope to stay that way until you decide otherwise—discretion is a must. Insist on preapproving your resume's travel itinerary, so it doesn't show up in the hands of your boss's golf partner. The more initial information you give to the recruiter, the easier it'll be for her to find the right fit for you.

If you can find two or three recruiters whom you trust and with whom you want to work, so much the better. Recruiters rely heavily on their personal contacts and arrangements with certain companies, so each recruiter widens your circle. But be careful not to make the circles so wide that they overlap. Recruiters may lose zeal to promote you if they send your resume to a company, only to find that another recruiter already did so. Tell your recruiters about one another so they have that information to work with.

"I make sure that I've introduced myself to those recruiting firms that do work in my field. I find out who they are by asking my target companies which recruiters they use. I register on the recruiter's website. I might even send a blind letter to introduce myself," says one job seeker. "If a recruiter sends around a query about a position that isn't right for me, I will try to find a way to help them identify a candidate who will be appropriate."

New York City's Ten Largest Search Firms

Rank	Firm	Specialties	Website
1	Response Cos.	Accounting, banking, marketing, healthcare	www.responseco.com
2	Solomon Page Group	Financial services, health care, life sciences	www.solomonpage.com
3	Spherion Corporation	Financial services, legal, tech	www.spherion.com
4	Forum Associates Inc	Accounting, advertising, human resources, IT	www.forumpersonnel.com
5	Execu/Search Group	Financial services, accounting, health care, HR	www.execu-search.com
6	Michael Page International	Banking, finance, accounting	www.michaelpage.com
7	Korn/Ferry International	Financial services, tech, life sciences	www.kornferry.com
8	Options Group	Financial services, tech, new media, e-commerce	www.optionsgroup.com
9	Russell Reynolds Associates	Financial services, manufacturing, health care, tech	www.russellreynolds.com
10	Mestel & Co.	Legal services	www.mestel.com

Other Large New York Recruiters

Firm	Specialties	Website
Heidrick & Struggles Intl.	Financial services, professional services, health care, tech	www.heidrick.com
Howard-Sloan Professional	Legal, financial	www.howardsloan.com
EJ Associates of New York	Hospitality, retail	www.ejassociates.com
DHR Intl. Executive Search	Retail, consumer products, financial services, tech, health care	www.dhrintl.net
A-L Associates	Financial services, tech, legal, operations	www.alassoc.com
Battalia Winston Intl.	Tech, manufacturing, health care, consumer products, financial services	www.battaliawinston.com
Koren, Rogers Associates	Financial services, HR, management, new media, e-commerce	www.korenrogers.com
Spencer Stuart	Consumer goods and services, financial services, industrial, life sciences, tech, media	www.spencerstuart.com
The Viscusi Group	Manufacturing: interior furnishings	www.viscusi.com
Wesley, Brown & Bartle Co.	Academia, aerospace, communications, health care, professional services, non-profit, manufacturing, financial services	www.wesleybrownbartle.com
Rhodes Associates	Real estate, financial services, health care	www.rhodesassociates.com
Global Research	Fortune 200 companies in all industries	www.globalresearchnet.com
Howard-Sloan-Koller Group	Media, advertising, entertainment	www.hsksearch.com
Gilbert Tweed Associates	Manufacturing, financial services, consumer, health care, legal, venture capital, tech	www.gilberttweed.com
Glocap Search	Tech, law, financial and investment services	www.glocap.com
Kenzer Corp.	Retail, manufacturing, financial services, hospitality, tech, consulting, health care	www.kenzer.com
OnPoint Partners	Insurance, financial services, health care	www.onpointpartners.com
Heath/Norton Associates	Management, engineering, sales/marketing	n/a
Hudson Highland Partners	Financial insurance, real estate, insurance	www.highlandsearch.com
Whitehead Mann Group	Communications, finance, HR, operations, legal, tech, sales/marketing	www.wmann.com

Source: *Crain's New York Business Book of Lists* 2006

WORKING WITH RECRUITERS

How can you best help the recruiter help you? The more you put into the process, the more you'll get out of it. Be honest and clear about your career goals. Describe the type of position you want, your salary requirements, where you want to work, and anything that is prima facie unacceptable. "The more I know about a candidate and what they are looking for," says one recruiter, "the more likely it is that I can make a great presentation about that person to a company."

Remember that you're the product the recruiter is selling. "Listen to the recruiter when it comes to interview technique and negotiation," says David Gomez, CEO of David Gomez and Associates, a Chicago-based recruiting agency specializing in marketing, advertising, accounting, finance, and diversity recruiting.

Recruiters send people out to interview all the time, and they get feedback afterward from both sides on what worked and what didn't. A good recruiter may be able to tell you the interviewing style of the person you'll be meeting, and perhaps even some of his or her trick questions. Even if you've spent a number of years in your field and know who you are and what you're worth, a recruiter can point out key details that will make your presentation of yourself more enticing to a potential employer.

REAL RECRUITER PROFILE

Industry: Information Technology
Region: New York City

What kinds of IT people do you place in New York?

I do recruiting primarily for Wall Street—commercial banks, investment banks.

Those companies are hiring very strongly for certain types of IT people. Half of our positions are Wall Street–related, and right now it's more like 75 percent. Wall Street is a gigantic user of technology professionals. The next highest is media, then consumer products, and a range of software developers.

What IT positions are in strongest demand?

In IT generally people can be broken into three broad categories:

1. Developers

2. Analysts, who understand what the business needs are, have liaison roles. They sit with business people and ask, "What do you need the computer to do? How can it work better?" Then they explain the needs to programmers.

3. Infrastructure people who support the systems, including network administrators

There is a fair amount of demand on all three fronts, but mostly [for] the analysts and project manager side—the people who understand the business. Partly, this is because of the offshore thing where the developers work from India where it's cheaper. The cost differential is vast. All the business people are here in New York. If the programmers are in Bangalore, it becomes all the more important that the specifications are right. It's like having a house built in India and shipped to you here. It's a different process than when it's built across the street and you can walk over and say, "I want a bedroom here and a bathroom there." The analyst is like the architect. He has to be very thorough and specific because if he isn't, he won't know until the house arrives and it has 12 doors and no bathroom."

Are New York companies continuing to outsource their technology needs?

There is a lot of offshoring going on, but it's not a blanket exodus. A fair amount of companies are pulling back. Although the cost is lower, the quality of the work they're getting is lousy—much is lost in translation, bad specs, not understanding the business, and the results they're getting are bad, so some of the offshore work is coming back.

What programming language is in most demand?

Java is still king. But even programmers who know Java must also know something about the business. It's not enough that they're top-notch programmers.

More and more companies are working very specialized. Even though they have an intense need to hire, they aren't being flexible. If you don't have 90 percent of what they specify, you don't even get an interview.

There is a herd mentality. On Wall Street especially, when one new financial offering is hot, they all want to jump into it. There is no mother lode because it's so new. As soon as a developer does a job in one company, he'll get snatched up by another for more money, and it goes on. They're fighting over a small group of people. And then something else gets hot and it starts all over.

Are companies paying sign-on bonuses?

For the certain people they want, they can be pretty generous. As we approach the end of the year, hiring companies know that the people they want are at companies that pay year-end bonuses. This is when the buying-out of bonuses occurs. In September some companies will buy out a candidate's year-end bonus.

Within financial services, where can IT people find the most work?

Many people think equities is where the business is, but on Wall Street equities pales compared to the amount of business done in fixed income. In global terms, the fixed income business is vastly bigger than the equity business. There is strong demand for those who know about bonds and loans and risk management.

Again, they want developers who know the fixed income business?

They're not willing to train in the knowledge base. They are not going to budge. You can be a great programmer, but if you don't have the specific business knowledge, you don't get the job. There are still a lot of people out there vying for jobs. If you have the special combination, the phone is ringing all the time for you. You have to have the bells and whistles on both the business and technical sides.

How do you find candidates to present to your clients?

Sometimes we look for candidates on Monster and HotJobs and Dice, but mostly we have our own internal database of candidates. I do a lot of networking. I call Paul and tell him what I need. He says talk to Frank who refers me to Susie.

NATIONAL RECRUITER NETWORKS

BankStaffers.com (www.bankstaffers.com)

National Association of Executive Recruiters (www.naer.org)

Oya's Directory of Recruiters (www.i-recruit.com)

Recruiters Online Network (www.recruitersonline.com)

Job Fairs

If you've ever been to a professional or industry conference, you can visualize the scene: rows of booths at which representatives of various employers are available to meet you, answer your questions, and accept your resume. Job fairs can be a useful way to make a personal contact within the companies on your interest list, but these meetings are not real interviews. Keep in mind that these representatives may speak with hundreds of job seekers while the fair is in session. You'll have only a brief opportunity to make an impression, so dress professionally and have a two-minute elevator pitch prepared about who you are and what you can offer.

Get a business card and follow up immediately afterward with an email, phone call, or written note reminding the recruiter of who you are. Your goal is to get a personal referral to the right hiring manager or, better yet, an interview. Beware, though: The people who staff job fair booths for a company are typically from the HR office. Your goal is to get to the hiring manager.

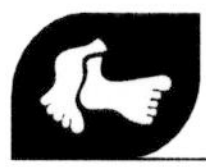

BE ENTHUSIASTIC

Whether you're making contact at a job fair, a networking session, or during an interview, one of the most effective things you can do to make a good impression is to show positive interest. Make eye contact, but avoid a stare down; ask good questions, but know when to listen as well; sit up straight toward the edge of your chair; and if you like what you hear, say so.

WHERE TO FIND JOB FAIRS

- Check the classified section of the *New York Times:* www.nytimes.com/pages/jobs/index.html.
- www.newyorkjobs.com/job_fair_calendar.cfm
- The New York State Department of Labor runs a listing of the current month's job fairs: http://www.labor.state.ny.us/careerservices/findajob/JobFairRecruitmentsIndex.shtm

Employment and Temp Agencies

"It's tough to make ends meet as an office temp," says an insider who temped for five months between jobs. "Plus it was stressful. You get a call around seven in the morning and you get suited up and go into the city. There were a lot of 'days of.'"

An employment agency can help place you in a job for a fee (sometimes that fee is paid by the employer). A temporary staffing agency helps companies fill short-term employment needs: filling in for employees on vacation or a leave of absence, or as extra hands for special projects. Some firms combine these functions by placing staff with employers for trial periods. If things work out, you convert to full-time employment after a specified period (and the employer pays a fee). If either you or the employer decide the job is not a good fit, you move on. What better way to get the real story on working conditions and job responsibilities?

A true temporary job (rather than a trial run for a full-time position) can provide the kind of flexibility you need when conducting a job search. Let your temp agency rep know you're looking for full-time work. With advance notice, you can schedule your assignments around job interviews.

NEW YORK CITY EMPLOYMENT AND TEMP AGENCIES

Access Staffing
360 Lexington Avenue, 8th Floor
New York, NY 10017
212-687-5440
www.accessstaffingco.com

Atrium
420 Lexington Avenue, Suite 1410
New York, NY 10170
212-292-0550
www.atriumstaff.com

Buckley Staffing
40 Exchange Place, Suite 1309
New York, NY 10005
212-344-9111
www.buckleystaffing.com

Careers on the Move
1120 Avenue of the Americas
New York, NY 10036
212-626-6889
www.careersonthemove.com

Custom Staffing
420 Lexington Avenue, Suite 550
New York, NY 10170
212-818-0300
www.customstaffing.com

Core Staffing
59 Maiden Lane
New York, NY 10038
212-766-1222
www.employcore.com

Hillary Taylor Personnel
2 John Street, 2nd Floor
New York, NY 10038
212-619-8200
www.hillarytaylor.com

Hire Counsel (legal)
575 Madison Avenue
New York, NY 10022
646-356-0550
www.hirecounsel.com

Madison Avenue Temporary Service for Communications
275 Madison Avenue, Suite 1314
New York, NY 10016
212-922-9040
www.matsforcommunications.com

Maximum Management Corp. (HR)
230 Park Avenue, Suite 635
New York, NY 10029
212-867-4646
www.maxmanhr.com

TemPositions
420 Lexington Avenue, 21st Floor
New York, NY 10170
212-490-7400
www.tempositions.com

Tempsations
Old Chelsea Station
P.O. Box 201
NY, New York 10011
212-255-9435
www.tempsations.net

United Staffing Systems
261 Madison Avenue, 2nd Floor
New York, NY 10016
212-743-0200
800-972-9725
www.unitedstaffing.com

Vance Staffing Services
12 East 41st Street, Suite 1301
New York, NY 10017
212-661-8860
www.vancestaffing.com

Networking

If you're an accountant, why not simply go to Monster.com and search for accounting/auditing jobs in New York City? Of the resulting 1,367 positions posted, you ought to land at least one job offer, right?

Wrong. A few hundred other accountants are also looking at those same postings. The minute a posting goes live, the hiring manager will be deluged with resumes. "I was amazed at the response," says a hiring manager who posted a temporary graphic design position on the popular publishing industry website, Media Bistro. "The emails began within minutes. We got more than 200 resumes, and this was for a job that would last two months! I had to find someone fast. I picked the first 20 that looked qualified and called five to interview. There was no way I could review 200 resumes."

You really need the inside track to find a good job. If you know the market is tight, keep your mind open and spread the word.

No matter how qualified you are, the odds are low that, even if you spend time crafting a compelling cover letter and tweaking the focus of your resume for each, your qualifications will stand out in the crowd. A better way to target your search is by talking to people working in your industry to find those job opportunities before they hit the classifieds. "The biggest thing is to tell everybody you're job hunting," says a New York job seeker who recently landed an IT job after a four-month search. "You really need the inside track to find a good job. If you know the market is tight, keep your mind open and spread the word."

RELATIONSHIPS MATTER

The adage "It's not what you know, it's who you know" couldn't possibly be more relevant than when it comes to a job search. We heard over and over that the way people learned about the job they landed was from a personal contact: former colleagues, friends of friends, the guy who sat next to them on a bus....

Networking can happen in a variety of ways. One job seeker said that when she learned that her employer was relocating to another state, she called everyone she knew and told them she was searching. "I've kept in touch with old colleagues from previous jobs and one of them had heard about this job. He told me who the key players were," she said. "He said I could use his name and then after the first interview, they spoke to him to see what his work experience was with me." She got the job.

Networking also includes aggressively pursuing people you've never met. One job seeker says, "When I'd read an article about somebody in the newspaper, I'd send them...a letter. I never got a response, but I figure this is like fishing. You've got to cast it out there."

Are there prominent members of a professional association that you admire? Seek them out and ask for an informational interview. Read professional journals and industry news articles. Contact the authors and let them know how their article was helpful. Just because there isn't a posted opening doesn't mean you shouldn't ask for a meeting. If you can get to know a person on a professional level, it's more likely that they'll think of you when a job becomes available, or when a recruiter calls them asking for a referral.

Talk to everyone. You never know where a tip will turn up. "I'd just moved to the city and at a poetry reading I talked to a girl sitting next to my friend. She said there was an opening at the literary agency where she worked," a job seeker in publishing told us. "That's how I found my temp agency, too. I volunteered at a music festival and told the girl that I was stuffing envelopes with that I needed a job. She told me about her temp agency."

THE GOLDEN RULE

Remember that what goes around, comes around. "It's important not only to ask how a person can help me, but also to do what I can to help someone else," says one job seeker. "If you ask for a favor you certainly should be willing to return it." One public relations professional regularly attends press briefings and sends a summary of the key points to her network of PR representatives who may not have had time to attend. Not only do her busy colleagues who need to keep up with their industry appreciate the service, it's also an opportunity to get her name in front of people who are most likely to know about jobs becoming available.

INFORMATIONAL INTERVIEWING

The networking process, properly executed, proceeds primarily through a series of information and referral meetings.

Information refers to the premise of the meeting, which is to exchange information and obtain advice—not, ostensibly, to interview for a specific job. By defusing the meeting in this way, you make it much easier for people to agree to meet with you.

Informational interviews are especially useful when you are changing careers and trying to break into a new industry. Informational interviews are not to be confused with job interviews. Rather they are where you gather valuable information that can lead you to some great referrals to people who are hiring or new resources for your current or future job searches.

When it comes to setting up informational interviews, find someone to talk to based on your interests and what you are targeting. This could be specific industries, companies, or a particular job function/role.

Use your networking skills to ask someone to agree to be "interviewed" by you for information. This can be done in person, by phone, or even an instant-messenger (IM) session if necessry. Prepare questions in advance. Try to connect with the person you're interviewing—research the field, industry, job function—to gain advice about your job search plan or next steps.

Informational Interview Etiquette

Keep the following points in mind during an informational interview:

- Keep your conversation targeted.
- Specifically ask for the information you want.
- Get names of contacts.
- Get out on time.

Sample Informational Interview Questions

Here are some questions to consider asking during an informational interview:

- Can you tell me a bit about your background?
- How did you get started in this industry?
- What's the company culture really like?
- Can you describe a typical day or week?
- What advice would you offer to someone trying to break into this industry?
- What do you like the most and least about the industry? About the job? About the company?
- How would you approach a job search for this organization or industry?
- Could you recommend other colleagues with whom I can speak? Can I use your name when I contact them?

INSIDER TIP

Contact your alumni association—especially if you went to school in New York City. Several insiders found research jobs through former professors. But even if you went to school in Denver, you might be surprised to find someone from the class of 1985 working in one of your targeted New York employers. Don't hesitate to ask for advice and perhaps even an introduction.

NETWORKING EVENTS

Networking events are one way to begin generating a circle of contacts and kick off your job search the right way. Not just for job seekers, networking events also provide a forum for generating new business and even making social contacts. There is typically an entry fee ranging from $10 to $35, depending on the forum. To get the most out of one of these events, attend not just as a job seeker, but rather with the simple intention of meeting new people. Chances are, you'll meet someone who works at, or knows someone who works at, one of your targeted employers.

Don't go into an organized networking event unprepared. While you probably won't deliver your two-minute presentation, you should know it cold. If you get into a conversation with someone, it will come out in just a couple of exchanges. It also helps to set goals, such as introducing yourself to at least ten people or making one contact with a live lead. You'll be surprised at how often you'll meet your goal without seeming to make much effort at all. It helps to be clear about the outcome you'd like.

Working a room is all about body language. Hold yourself with confidence, make eye contact, and shake hands. Take it easy on the alcohol, and don't ramble on in conversations—*the ability to listen makes a great first impression.* If you're nervous, pretend you're the host and your job is to go around making sure your guests feel comfortable. Follow through promptly on any promises you make to email information or make phone calls. Remember, if you provide a favor to someone, it's easier to call him when you need the favor returned.

Finding New York City Networking Events

Acquaint New York—A.N.Y. (www.acquaintnewyork.com)

Association of the Bar of the City of New York (www.abcny.org)

Career Journal (www.careerjournal.com/calendar/newyork.html)

Exécutifs 212—NY organization of French-speaking executives (www.executifs212.org)

Five O'Clock Club (www.fiveoclockclub.com)

J2J Network—NY network for Jewish professionals (www.j2jnetwork.org)

Manhattan Chamber of Commerce (www.manhattancc.org/events)

Media Bistro (www.mediabistro.com/events)

Networking for Professionals (www.networkingforprofessionals.com)

New York State Society of CPAs (www.nysscpa.org)

New York Women in Communications (www.nywici.org)

Netparty (www.netparty.com)

Ryze—membership required (www.ryze.com)

Women Sports Jobs (www.womensportsjobs.com)

WorldWIT—Women in Technology (www.worldwit.org/Events2.aspx)

Landing a Job

First Steps

Now that you know where to look for jobs, you can concentrate on how to present yourself in the best light. Finding a job in New York City is fundamentally no different from finding a job anywhere else. The process simply has a broader scope. (Take a job search in any other city and multiply by ten.) Some would also say the stakes are higher. The competition is stiff; the cost of living is through the ceiling. How long can you live on your savings or severance pay? You have to work smart, set priorities, be persistent, and stay positive. And this means developing a thorough job-search plan and sticking to it.

GET ORGANIZED

Just as you would for a class or any major project, record your goals and track your progress in a dedicated notebook or in a folder on your computer that's just for your job search. As your search evolves, it will be very helpful to be able to refer to your notes to see what you've done, what worked, what didn't, and so on.

When conducting online research, organize the sites you review regularly in your Internet browser's "Favorites" or "Bookmarks" list, so that you don't waste time trying to find information you've already located.

How much time should you spend on your job search each week?

- If you're in school, plan to devote as much time to your job search as you would to a single course.
- If you're looking for a job while employed, plan to spend 15 hours per week on your search.
- If you're unemployed, treat your search as if it were a full-time job. Devote 35 hours per week to the effort.

ASSESS YOURSELF

> **I have to remind myself that finding the right position takes a marathon, not a sprint. Concentrating on day-to-day accomplishments helps.**

Any good job search begins with a thorough self-assessment. Looking for a new job is a great opportunity to realign your goals—and it's up to you to articulate exactly what those goals are.

Start by asking yourself these questions and spend some time reflecting on the answers:

- What are my values? Deep down, what guides me as I make my decisions? Is it a need to make a difference or make big bucks, be the center of attention or help others?
- What are my priorities and objectives for the next few years? What about five years from now?
- What are my core strengths?
- What provides meaning in my life? What is my purpose?
- Where does work fit into my vision of life?

To really get the most out of this exercise, and those that follow, write out or type up your thoughts in a notebook or computer document. Doing so will force you to crystallize your ideas and make it possible for you to refer to them later.

Finding the answers to these questions now will make the next steps of your job search much easier, and the final result a greater success by landing you in a position that is as closely aligned as possible with your goals.

DEFINE YOUR GOALS

Maybe you know exactly what type of job you want, but don't know which employers look for your skills? Or maybe you're interested in a particular industry because you want to make a difference or make a lot of money, but don't know where to look for employers. (To follow our example, pharmaceutical companies and investment banks employ a range of people with nonscientific and nonfinancial backgrounds.) Or maybe you want to make new use of your experience (a manufacturing executive who moves into consulting, for instance). Getting a grip on your priorities will help you focus your search and avoid wasting time pursuing irrelevant leads.

INSIDER TIP

Do something else in your daytime. When I worked on my job search all day, it was so discouraging," says a job seeker. "I started playing squash. It was great to get out and do something different, especially something physical."

Let's say you're an MBA interested in management consulting. Will you look at the elite corporations? Those affiliated with Big Four accounting firms? Or will you consider smaller boutique companies? Or perhaps you're a human resources generalist. In what industry will you search? What size company? What about an HR consulting firm or an executive search firm? If you're interested in working in New York City, do you want an office location in Manhattan? Or will you consider a position across the Hudson River in New Jersey? The answers to these questions will help you define your search in a way that can make it more manageable.

Consider this: It takes a field of 200 possible positions to produce one job offer. You may have a particular company in mind that you'd like to work for, but to generate three good offers (a reasonable goal), you will need to define your search more broadly.

To broaden your target, consider how your background in one industry might be relevant in another. For instance, publishers of educational books and materials often look for individuals with teaching experience. An HR professional with experience in financial services and a specialty in employee benefits who wants to find a job in Manhattan may consider several targets based on her skills and experience:

- Employee benefits manager at a top-tier investment bank (an advancement consistent with profession and industry experience)
- Employee benefits manager for a health services organization (to explore using professional qualifications in a new industry)
- Account representative for a consulting firm specializing in employee benefits (a different use of professional skills and experience)
- Group insurance sales representative for a health insurance company (to develop a new ability in a related career option)

RESEARCH YOUR TARGET INDUSTRIES AND COMPANIES

Make a list of your job options (similar to the list above) based on how you fit into the industries, organizations, and roles that interest you. Focus on a maximum of two or three industries and select 10 to 20 organizations for your top priority list. Choose another ten organizations for your backup plan.

Consider these questions as you research careers and industries:

- What product or service does this industry offer?
- Who are the major players and up-and-comers?
- What are the critical success factors for a company in the industry?
- What is the outlook and hiring potential for this industry?
- What type of talent does the industry attract and hire?

While researching companies, ask yourself:

- What differentiates this company from others in the industry?
- What are this company's culture, values, and priorities?
- Who are its leaders (CEO, CFO, and COO), and what do they seem to stand for?

- How does this company treat its employees?
- What is the company's reputation?
- What would it be like to work there?

INSIDER TIP

Midcareer job seekers should expect to spend one to two months searching for every $10,000 of salary. For example, a job paying $80,000 could take 8 to 16 months to find.

Based on what you learned in the second chapter and the additional research you've done, start with the list of targets you made from the two or three industries and 20 or so organizations that interest you, and sketch out your plan of attack. Where will you look for job postings and how often? How will you tap your network to find industry and company contacts?

Contacts can provide information and other contacts. They can help you decide if your goals are reasonable. Manhattan may not be the best place for an aerospace engineer to find a job, for instance. Or maybe on further investigation, you decide you don't want to work for MTV after all. Contacts can also get you closer to your goal of targeting an available job.

DEVELOP A SELF-MARKETING STRATEGY

When it comes down to it, what is a job search really? You're essentially trying to develop a business relationship with an employer, to sell them your services: the skills and experience that you bring to a job. And any service or product needs promotion to sell. So think about your job search as a marketing campaign to sell your number-one product...you. To help plan your marketing strategy, think of yourself in terms of the classic marketing five Ps:

Product: What do you have to offer? What key skills and attributes can you offer your "customers" (that is, potential employers)?

Price: What is your value in the marketplace? Do your education, experience, and strengths qualify you as a premium product—something elite—or will you need to be "discounted" to get your foot in the door of your target industry?

Promotion: What themes or messages convey what you have to offer professionally?

Place (distribution): How will you distribute yourself on the market? Consider using multiple means of "delivering" yourself to potential employers. This could include on-campus recruiting events, job ads, career fairs, company websites, executive recruiters, and referrals from your network.

Positioning: What differentiates you from other candidates? What is unique about your skills, background, or interests?

Use your answers to these questions to help create your resume and cover letters and to fashion your pitches to contacts and potential employers. You'd be surprised at how effective a well-targeted job marketing campaign can be. If you know exactly how your product meets an employer's needs, the sell will be much easier.

To build a resume in a new field, try working in a temporary capacity or at a nonprofit.

Your Resume and Cover Letter

Your resume and cover letter are tools that will help you get an interview. A strong, well-constructed document is the baseline: the minimum requirement for a job search. A poorly prepared document can and will work against you. In the competitive employment market of New York City, busy managers and others who might screen your resume are looking for a way to narrow the list of choices. Something as seemingly insignificant as a single-letter typo can get your resume tossed into the trash.

Before you begin writing your resume you must scrutinize yourself. Which elements of your years of wisdom, experience, and accomplishment belong on a single sheet of paper, and which don't? What kind of candidate does your target firm usually hire? This is where all of your previous self-assessment and prioritizing will really be put to use.

A complete discussion of how to prepare winning cover letters and resumes is beyond the scope of this book. Consider supplementing the advice here with one of WetFeet's resume guides: *Killer Cover Letters and Resumes!*, *Killer Consulting Resumes!*, or *Killer Investment Banking Resumes!*

NEWS FLASH: A RESUME WON'T GET YOU A JOB

At best, a resume will get you an interview. At worst, it will get you eliminated from consideration. So make sure your resume is flawless, and see it for what it really is: a marketing tool to present your qualifications to potential employers, in consideration of a future business relationship.

RESUME TIPS

Know Thy Audience

We can't stress enough the need to do due diligence on the firms you're targeting. Almost every firm will ask the question, "Why us?" Make sure you can give an informed answer to this question. Think about what, specifically, might appeal to the recruiting team at your chosen firm. You may choose to include a reference in the cover letter. Look into the firm's noted areas of strength and focus, find out in which industries or product areas it excels. All of this information should influence your resume and cover letter, and especially the way in which you pursue an interview. Most firms have a website you can quickly check for some basic information. "With the Internet making it easy to access information, there's no reason to go to an interview without knowing an incredible amount of information," says a recruiter.

Because resumes must be tailored to the audience to be successful, you will often need to prepare different versions of your resume for different positions and companies. It is well worth your time to do so. After all, you only have one chance to make a first impression. If you're applying for positions in several industries, it may make sense to have several versions of your resume (one tailored to each industry) ready to go.

COMMON GROUND

Resume reviewers look favorably on candidates with backgrounds similar to their own. Read the employee profiles included in many firms' recruiting materials and websites and find someone who worked in the same company or attended the same school you did. You'll have a better chance of getting a favorable review.

Know Thyself

In addition to knowing all the factual information about yourself—grades, test scores, and so on—you need to think about how to portray yourself in a positive, confident light while telling the true story of who you are and what you've accomplished. You must have a good deal of insight into your experience, strengths, and weaknesses to create a compelling resume. Some of the many sources of inspiration for this include:

- Academic records
- Employment history
- Performance reviews
- Recommendations
- Top accomplishments

A Note About Contact Information

Your name and contact information are the most important things to supply to an employer, and they should head the pages of all resumes. Seems straightforward, but many people make the mistake of sending resumes with old contact information or omitting telephone numbers and email addresses. Be sure to include the name you use professionally, a home address, the telephone number or numbers where you are most easily reached, and a professional-sounding email address (no "gothgirl81@yahoo.com"—don't laugh, we've seen email addresses just like this one on many resumes).

It's a numbers game. "Basically you need to send out a lot of applications. You need to target your letter to the job if you want to get an interview," says a management consulting insider. "A lot of people don't seem to know that."

COVER LETTERS

The cover letter should be kept short and to the point, never more than one page. Don't rely on your cover letter to fill in the gaps or to put a customized spin on your experience. It's important that all your critical information be contained in your resume, because there's a good chance that your cover letter won't be read. The cover letter should include the reason you're interested in the company and the highlights of your experience that make you a good candidate for that company. If you have a contact at the company, mention that person.

Avoid "canned" letters! Recruiters and hiring managers tell us that formulaic letters often end up in the "no" pile. The applicant who customizes his words is more appealing and will be given preference over others. One insider puts it this way: "The cover letter is the one opportunity they have to talk to me." Employers don't want to waste their time on a candidate who is not genuinely interested in the position and their company.

INSIDER TIP

"It pays to be proactive and actually call as opposed to emailing. I wouldn't have gotten the interview if I hadn't called," says one job seeker. "Of course, if their ad says 'don't call,' then don't call."

And finally, put the same care into preparing your cover letter when submitting your resume via email. The ease and informality of email can be deceiving, so don't forget to include a cover letter.

KEEPING IT ALL ORGANIZED

Be sure to keep a copy of every resume and cover letter you send out on your computer, clearly labeled with the company and job title. When you are asked to come in for an interview, you will need to bring copies of your resume with you. You'll also want to review your cover letter and resume before the interview to ensure that your interview presentation is consistent with your application.

And online job postings often disappear as quickly as they appear, so we recommend copying and pasting the postings into a document on your computer. If you are called in for an interview, you will certainly want to refresh your memory. And sometimes, those calls may come a month or more after you submitted a resume, making it very difficult to recall the details of an individual job opening.

Searching from Out of Town

"The most difficult thing is that I didn't have a job when I was looking for a job," says a job seeker who moved to New York from the West Coast. "I didn't use my local contacts enough before I moved. I figured that if they didn't work for a New York company, they wouldn't be able to help. Thinking back, I could have leveraged my territory more. You never know what connections they might have. I could have set up my search long-distance and perhaps even had a job before I arrived."

Landing a job in the city isn't impossible for those who don't yet live here. It is more difficult, however, and it will require even more organization and tenacity than a local job search. The from-a-distance job search is somewhat easier for recent and soon-to-be graduates (as opposed to those currently employed in another city), since recruiters know that many students move to New York City after graduation. Those who are currently or recently employed in another city will have the burden of proof—you will have to convince hirers that you are serious about moving to New York. Recruiting is a time-consuming and expensive undertaking, and recruiters are wary of wasting time on applicants who aren't serious. You mustn't appear to be testing the water. Be sure to highlight any evidence of your commitment to moving to New York City: if you have ties to the city (for example, family) or you have lived here in the past, say so!

A letter-writing campaign can be particularly effective for an out-of-town search. Indicate that you are planning a trip to the city on certain dates and call back to set up interviews during these dates. Try to group your meetings into a two- or three-day schedule and plan several such visits to the city. In this way, you'll maximize your time until you can develop a lead willing to pay for your interview trip. If you come to New York for a two-week stay without doing this homework, your trip will very likely be a waste of time and money. Not to mention a drain on your enthusiasm.

These short trips can also be a good chance to explore the city and decide whether this is really somewhere you want to live. If you're a teacher, for instance, can you afford to live in Manhattan? Or will you be willing to commute in from less expensive digs in Queens, Brooklyn, or Jersey City?

RELOCATION CONCERNS

New York City is the most expensive city in the United States (and ranks 12th worldwide after Tokyo, London, Hong Kong, Copenhagen, Seoul, and Geneva.) It's 13 percent more expensive than Los Angeles, 15 percent higher than Chicago, and 16 percent higher than San Francisco, according to a 2004 study by Mercer. But don't expect an equivalent increase in your salary. According to Salary.com's Cost-of-Living Wizard, NYC employers typically pay 0.8 percent less than San Francisco employers! To compare the cost-of-living differential between your city and New York, go to http://swz.salary.com/CostOfLivingWizard/layoutscripts/coll_start.asp.

Whether you can expect your prospective employer to pay for your move to the city depends primarily on the relative scarcity of your skill set, and secondarily on the industry and company in question. The higher the demand for your skills, the higher the likelihood that a company will consider offering you a relocation bonus. The average relocation bonus is in the range of $3,000 to $8,000. Relocation allowances are more common for MBAs and other advanced-degree holders in the investment banking and management consulting industries and for management professionals with industry experience—especially those who are being recruited away from a competitor.

Real Job Seeker Profile

Position: public relations
Industry: financial services
Length of job search: five months

How many hours per week do you spend on your search?

I spend at least eight hours a day, mostly on weekdays, but sometimes I'll do things on weekends.

How do you structure your days?

I work at least nine to five just like anyone would in a regular business setting.

Aren't you tempted to take a little time to relax and have fun?

Of course, but I save that for evenings and weekends, just as I had done when I was working.

What does a typical day look like?

Every morning I go and work out first thing. Then I come back and read the *New York Times* and the *Wall Street Journal* between 8:00 and 8:00. For the next hour I'll check my email. I make most of my phone calls between 10 and noon, although there are certainly times that I have to return phone calls in the afternoon. It's more productive to get the phone calls in at the beginning of the day. I always try to take a lunch break. Sometimes I'll have set up a lunch appointment. I try to set up interviews and meetings around lunch.

At any rate, I try to get out every day, even if it's for a walk. The afternoon is when I'm usually writing follow-up and thank-you letters, or doing research to target people I want to network with for positions that are open.

How do you use the Internet for research?

I will go on any and all job search websites—I'll do Monster, CareerJournal.com, trade organization websites, corporate websites. I have a target list of 50 different companies, so I cycle through those on a regular basis and check for appropriate openings.

Do you respond to the job listings by applying online or by email? Or do you try to contact someone directly inside the company?

Both. At a minimum it's good to apply online, but there are so many people that do that, I think it's important to take additional steps to make sure you get called in for an interview.

How many interviews have you gotten?

I do at least one job interview a week on average, which is a lot.

How do you get so many?

I'm a big believer in networking. I started with the people I know. I made a marketing plan that identified what I want to do and where I want to do it. I identified 50 companies that I think are places where I might want to work. I try to talk to people that I know who might know people at those companies that I can chat with.

Do you ask for an introduction? Or do you ask if you can use his or her name when you make the call?

Whichever they're most comfortable with. I'll tell you about the latest one. I saw an opening for one of my targeted companies on its website, so I applied online. But I also did research on the company website to guess, really, who might be the hiring manager. Then I looked at the background of the hiring manager and identified a previous company where I knew someone. It took me at least a month and a half to even get in the door because my contact at the other company was traveling. But once I was able to get hold of him, he offered to make the call himself. He was the CEO—that's kind of unusual. These people are generally pretty busy. I got an interview!

Are there professional groups that are especially good for networking in your industry?

Since I'm looking at financial PR, I look at both the financial community and the public relations community. I belong to the Financial Women's Association and the PR Society of America. I also attend other communication organization meetings.

Is there a particular New York source that is helpful?

Not New York–based, other than people. I just think that you need to do everything and anything in a job search that's legal. Always use a wide mix of different activities.

What's the wildest thing you've done in your job search?

I think talking the CEO into calling someone for me was probably the furthest I've extended myself. He was somebody that wanted to hire me for a position and that didn't work out. I just had a feeling that there was a reserve of goodwill—that I had built a strong enough relationship. You don't always ask a CEO for things like that.

Have you considered working with an executive recruiter or search firm?

I do that on a regular basis.

How do you make contacts? Do recruiters find you?

Sometimes they call me and sometimes I call them. First, I make sure that I've introduced myself to those recruiting firms that do work in my field. I find out who they are by asking my target companies which recruiters they use. I register on recruiters' websites. I might even send a blind letter into a recruiting firm to introduce myself. If a recruiter sends around a query about a position that isn't right for me, I will try to find a way to help them identify a candidate who will be appropriate. It's a lot of work, but it could pay off, so I do it.

How do you dress for interviews?

I still believe in suits. Yes, I've been overdressed, but the first impression is a lasting one. It's better to err on the conservative side.

What gets better results: email or telephone?

I use both. I'll email initially—a lot of people are most comfortable with that. Then I alternate. If I don't hear back from the email, I'll make a phone call. If I don't get a response from a phone call, I'll go back to email. I'll make at least six different overtures to get a meeting with someone. Usually you don't have to do that much.

Five months is a long time to be working full-time at finding a job. How do you stay positive?

First of all I believe that I'm going to get a new and exciting job. I truly believe that. It's just a matter of being in the right time and right place. Also, I've done some freelancing to keep things interesting and moving along. Actually, five months of searching is not a lot. The rule is that for every $10,000 you want to make, it takes a month of hunting.

Job hunting is always frustrating. But I meet enough really nice people along the way and I get encouraging feedback. Also, I'm a positive person. That's just my bent. But I do think people genuinely want to help each other. So there's a kind of natural kindness that comes across.

The biggest obstacle for me in a job search is overcoming impatience. I have to remind myself that finding the right position takes a marathon, not a sprint. Concentrating on day-to-day accomplishments helps.

Put Your Best Foot Forward

GETTING TO THE INTERVIEW...ON TIME

Congratulations! You got the meeting. You've done a Mapquest search to learn the exact location, and you'll be there on the dot at the appointed time. Sounds easy.

But remember that this is New York City. You can get practically anywhere you need to go on public transportation. But if something can go wrong, it likely will—especially when you're on a tight schedule. Allow extra time for police actions in the subway, a taxi stuck in traffic, or for walking the wrong way from Sixth Avenue and ending up on Seventh instead of Fifth.

Barring complications, the subway is remarkably reliable and definitely the cheapest way to get from point A to point B, especially if you're moving in a straightforward north/south direction. You can plan your subway route online at www.HopStop.com. Your MetroCard works on city buses as well, but since they travel on the surface rather than underground, they're subject to traffic tangles. Frankly, it's often faster to walk. However, express buses can be very helpful in (cheaply) reaching places the subway does not.

Taxicabs aren't the luxury in New York that they are elsewhere. They're a reliable and well-used form of transport; but beware—the cost can add up. A quick ride is easily $6 and more often $10 to $12, plus tip. And try to avoid shift turnover hours when every advancing cab has its off-duty sign illuminated. But a taxi ride to an occasional important meeting is the best way to increase your chances of arriving in your most fresh, unfrazzled condition and (not a small thing) at the exact location of your destination.

And if you're foolish enough to drive in Manhattan, well...good luck with that. Seriously, people do drive in the city (how else could the traffic be so heavy?). But unless you know the city well, are accustomed to driving offensively, and know exactly where you'll be able to park during your appointment, keep the car in reserve for a day when timing is not an issue.

WHAT TO WEAR

When in doubt, go conservative. If you fear you may be overdressed in a business suit at a company that favors T-shirts and shorts (hint: not many New York companies maintain a workplace this casual, but at some, business casual rules), you might phone the company's front desk and ask how employees generally dress. If your route requires you to walk any distance, wear comfortable walking shoes (ladies, that's why women in New York seem to always carry a bag—it's for their great-looking shoes). You don't want to be distracted by the throbbing of a big fat blister when you should be concentrating on describing your past accomplishments.

Consider the type of work you're interviewing for when deciding what to wear. Those in more creative professions are usually expected to dress a little less formally and a little more creatively.

DRESS COMMENSURATE WITH EXPERIENCE

Your experience and the level of the job you are applying for will also affect your ideal mode of dress. For an entry-level candidate, the objective is to come across as capable and mature. A midcareer candidate, on the other hand, may want to accentuate his or her adaptability to a new office culture by foregoing the generic corporate uniform.

The Basics

Always a lady. Recruiters of all stripes seem to agree that a candidate can't go wrong with a well-tailored suit in a neutral color (black, navy, and gray are your best bets). At more conservative companies—such as investment banks, consulting firms, and law firms—a skirt suit is de rigueur, and anything other than nontextured nude hose and heels is pushing the envelope of what's acceptable. Otherwise, a tasteful pantsuit with medium-heeled leather loafers will look put-together and professional. If ironing stresses you out, a silk or fine-gauge wool sweater shell can replace a button-down shirt and remain wrinkle-free under a suit. Oh, and minimal makeup and nonflashy jewelry, please.

For the guys. For men, a suit in a dark, neutral color, a white or blue dress shirt, and a silk tie in a conservative pattern should do just fine for most interviews. Stick to natural fabrics, like wool and cotton. "Well-heeled" generally implies a pair of polished, not ground-down-at-the-heels leather shoes in black. Beyond that, wingtips send a more conservative signal, while shoes with lug or platform soles are more funky than professional. Don't fall victim to the white-socks-with-dress shoes syndrome that plagues many unfortunate men, and be sure that your trouser socks pass the elasticity test, so that they don't sag around your ankles midway through your interview (along with your chances of landing the job).

A NOTE ON THE WEATHER

For most of the year New York City is either too hot or too cold. If it's hot outdoors, count on frigid interiors, and vice versa. Plan your layers accordingly. On those famously humid days of summer, you'll want to plan for a rest stop to freshen up before your meeting.

Real Hiring Manager Profile

Industry: Magazine Publishing

How do you determine which candidates to interview?

It's a combination of three different elements: the cover letter, the resume, and a sample of work. We want somebody who shows us in the cover letter they've bothered to read the ad. Somebody who actually responded to the ad's criteria and said, "I've done this and I have experience in that." Simply sending a resume and a three- or four-line formulaic cover that says "I'm responding to your ad on X and attached is my resume"—that is not going to work. It doesn't send a good signal.

What kind of mistakes do you see in cover letters?

My name is listed in the ad. This is a marvelous way to sort. Many of the cover letters start out with "Dear hiring manager." That tells me they hadn't read carefully and weren't really that interested. The other mistake is that for the position of art director, five people applied for a creative director position. You have to apply for the position available even if your skills exceed it.

How do you prefer candidates submit their application?

Email is fine, but there are problems with it. We are comfortable using it for everything, and we don't shift gears when we use it professionally. Make sure your cover letter is as professional as if you were mailing it as a letter. Email is a medium intended for a quick response. You shouldn't be sending your resume from a Blackberry.

What about the resume?

Cleanness and readability. It's very important to see a chronological sequence. You can use a top-line summary of your experience and skills if you like, but follow it with a chronological sequence of jobs. If you omit the year you graduated from college, that's a problem.

But people do that to avoid age-discrimination.

I don't have a problem with someone who is very senior in the field. Maybe it seems they are too qualified, too experienced for our position. If they make a strong enough point about why this job is everything they've dreamed of, or that they want to work in a close-knit environment—whatever. But it they come right out and address it, it's going to help a lot. It's very hard to ignore a letter like that even if the person is very senior. You just put yourself at a disadvantage if you conceal that you're over 40. It's a ridiculous unfair world, but you can do it.

How does someone get their resume noticed?

I look at every one. We had a case where I had eliminated a resume because of a typo. The guy then wrote to me and reminded me that we used to work together. I remembered him and brought him in to interview. It never hurts to know someone. You can't hesitate. Also if someone I know tells me this is a person I really should look at, that's compelling.

What about interns?

Many of our interns now work for other magazines published by our parent company. They made the contacts here. They also impressed me and I made the recommendation when an opening came up. It's important to do throughout your career. Not always as an intern. You can volunteer. Make contacts. Interning is for many reasons a very good thing to do.

How do you prefer that people follow up?

I really do care about getting a thank-you note. Especially with interns. This is not a joke. It's a problem for me. Whether the interview is by phone or in person. Email will do, or the traditional way, either handwritten or typed. If you interview with two people, you have to write thank-you notes to both.

What other mistakes do people make?

I disqualify people who haven't had the courtesy to look at the magazine—or at materials for this place you're applying to. Clicking on the website is not enough. If you don't know who the editor-in-chief is, that's not okay. Even more important: Don't tell me you've read the magazine if you haven't. I'm not joking. This is for real.

What happens in the interview?

For one thing, it's better if you listen than talk. If you're asked a question, you should answer it, of course. But it's really good to answer the question and let the person ask you another. I see it with interns especially—compulsive self-centered talking. I don't entirely care about you. I care about what you can do for me. Sometimes it's a symptom of nerves. The challenge is figuring out if they're nervous or impossible.

IN THE INTERVIEW

Companies use interviews to get to know candidates and to see how they might fit into the workplace. Although better than relying on resumes alone, interviews are an inexact process, carried out differently in different organizations and groups within organizations. There are, however, several basic approaches that you are likely to encounter. Understanding these approaches will help you devise effective interview strategies, increase your confidence, and make a better impression on your interviewers.

NEWS FLASH: YOU'RE AN INTERVIEWER, TOO

The goal of an interview is not to get a job offer, but to gather information. You should be assessing potential employers in the same way they're assessing you. Not only does asking intelligent questions about the job give you a better picture of what you're stepping into, it also makes a great impression by showing that you're serious about the job.

In general, you can expect to be asked about items on your resume that may be unclear or in which the interviewer is particularly interested. This type of questioning, along with questions about your career goals and expectations of your employer, fall under the category we call clarification interviewing. A few interviewers will ask only these kinds of questions—indicating, perhaps, inexperience, lack of interest in learning much about you, or fear of turning you off with more challenging questions.

Usually, however, you will also be asked doubt-resolving questions, which might address why you left your last job, what you see as your greatest weaknesses, and why the job appeals to you. Many interviewers will limit themselves to just clarification and doubt-resolving questions—but some will not.

Interviewers may also use techniques designed to determine how you would operate on the job—such as questioning you about how you have responded to certain types of situations in the past (behavioral interviewing) or how you think you would respond to a given hypothetical situation or set of facts (hypothetical situations and case analysis); putting you into a simulated or real on-the-job situation (audition interviewing); making you uncomfortable to test your reaction to pressure (stress interviewing); or having a psychologist delve into your past experiences, motivations, and influences (psychological interviewing).

One insider told us about a company that interviewed a group of candidates all at once. "We went in as a group and they would escort people out one by one. Then there were two of us left. They see how you interact, how you deal with group dynamics." He got the job. "A lot of the other candidates weren't prepared for the interview. They didn't know why they wanted to work for that company or what the company does," he says. "I didn't really push because I'm not like that. Yeah, you need to make sure you're heard, but not come off too aggressive. Of course, they might be looking for an aggressive person. But that's not how I did it."

The following interview approaches are common:

- **Clarification** questions aim to achieve greater understanding of what you claim in your resume as your education, experience, or accomplishments, as well as your goals and expectations of your manager or the company.
- **Doubt-resolving** questions aim to resolve possible concerns or doubts about your judgment, veracity, behavior, or achievements.
- **Behavioral** questions aim to learn whether you have encountered challenges similar to those anticipated and how you handled them.
- **Hypothetical** questions aim to test whether your thinking and judgment are likely to be appropriate for the on-the-job challenges you might encounter.
- **Case analysis** aims to test whether you can comprehend a complex set of facts, create a framework for analyzing them, and arrive at logical and useful conclusions.
- **Auditioning** aims to watch your actual behavior in a simulated or real on-the-job situation.
- **Stress** interviews aim to test your reactions to pressure to see whether you keep your cool or lose it.
- **Psychological** interviews aim to determine the major influences on your reasoning and your emotions, in order to predict how you might perform under a variety of circumstances or management approaches.

For in-depth advice on handling these kinds of questions and more, check out WetFeet's *Ace Your Interview!*

Follow Up Effectively

Remember, the purpose of an interview is to gather information. The job offer itself is made during follow-up.

It's customary to send a brief and personal thank-you note (email is fine) after an interview. Don't be shy about phoning or emailing at the agreed-on time. But follow-up is also more than simply a status check. In fact, it could be the most important step in the entire job search process.

If you've ever had sales training, it can really pay off at this stage of your job search. What you may not know is that the hiring manager uses the interview process to sharpen his concept of what he is looking for. (He may not understand this either, but it happens, nonetheless.) Each candidate he meets with will change the job description somewhat. In your follow-up, it would be smart to ask if the definition of the job has changed since you spoke. You can also ask what other people he is considering and what they have to offer that you don't. Or, simply ask: What kind of person is the ideal candidate and how do I compare? During this stage, you are a salesperson. That means you must seek out every objection and address it. Your goal is to show the hiring manager that you can fill this newly defined need better than your competition.

Salary Concerns

New Yorkers love to talk about money, but not in the context of a job interview. As New York recruiter Sunny Bates says, "The rule of the salary game is the first to name a figure loses." As she points out, the right time to talk salary is when you're certain the company wants to offer you a job. If you bring it up too early, you may appear to be more interested in money than in what you can offer the company. However, if you wait too long, you might waste valuable time pursuing an offer from a company whose salary range is below your expectations.

KNOW YOUR WORTH IN THE NEW YORK JOB MARKET

There are several ways to research salary levels. Some representative salaries are included in this book, but you'll want to supplement this information with your own research, since company size and job descriptions influence salary levels. You can also find salaries and job descriptions at Salary.com, www.nyjobsource.com, and other career and job information sites. The New York Department of Labor also has representative salary data.

If you're asked to provide your salary history, be prepared to provide it, along with any relevant information about your expectations. For example, if your last salary was much lower than you're expecting to earn in New York City, note that the cost of living was much lower and that you expect your new salary to reflect that difference.

NEGOTIATION BASICS

Many people see negotiation as a process whereby each party tries to get the most for what they have to give. And that's a reasonable way to look at it when you're buying or selling a car, a computer, or a carpet. It's tempting to look at job negotiations in the same way—but not advisable.

We offer a quick gloss on the compensation negotiation here, but for the full story, check out the WetFeet Insider Guide to *Negotiating Your Salary & Perks*.

Shoot for Fair

When you're negotiating an employment contract, you're negotiating the basis for a relationship, and you want to live happily together. This doesn't mean that you have to arrive at a compromise, but that you should come to an agreement that both parties feel is fair.

There are at least four factors that can increase your perceived worth. All of them fit into the context of networking and interviewing, and all of them can be turned to your advantage without alienating potential employers.

1. How you see and present yourself. Are you confident? Do you speak convincingly about your accomplishments? Do you have a clear and credible objective? Do you understand and seem to fit in with the company's culture? You will generate more buyer enthusiasm if the company sees you as a long-term asset than if it sees you only as right for this particular job.

2. How the company values the work to be done. This is your opportunity to put the work in a broader context than the company may see. Instead of talking about providing good customer service, for example, you might discuss retaining valued customers and increasing business activity. If you present some convincing illustrations, the job might seem worthy of a higher valuation—including, perhaps, a bonus for achieving objectives that you help define.

3. The company's perception of your appropriateness for the job. You want to demonstrate that what you've learned and achieved in the past, along with your understanding of the company's needs, makes you more qualified than other candidates.

4. Your discussion of compensation and benefits. Your attention to the first three factors should already have raised the company's estimation of your value. The direct discussion—often thought of as the whole of negotiation—is where you apply your skills at recapitulation, listening, and politely asserting the value you have established.

Benefits

IMPROVING A LOW-BALL OFFER

One way to deal with a low salary is to upgrade the job. In your discussion, try to show the hiring manager how your experience and knowledge can accommodate extra responsibilities. Cover this before talking about salary. You'll know if the job duties are below your level.

The range of benefits you can expect from an NYC employer varies greatly depending primarily on industry practices and company size. At a minimum, for a full-time position, you should expect to be offered health insurance, although you may have to contribute as much as half the cost, and a vacation package. A 401(k) retirement plan is also common, but your employer may or may not make a contribution on your behalf. Family leave is a federally mandated benefit, but it may be unpaid. However, the State of New York provides short-term disability benefits; your employer might also provide long-term disability insurance.

Other benefits that may be included:

- Tuition assistance
- Adoption assistance
- Health club membership

- Dental insurance
- Life insurance
- Vision insurance
- Child and elder care assistance
- Sabbaticals/leaves of absence
- Matching charitable contributions
- Flexible spending account
- Employee assistance plan

Final Words

YOU LANDED THE JOB! NOW WHAT?

Get ready for the realities of business life in this center of commerce and industry. NYC employers are savvy users of limited resources. Your workspace may be as claustrophobic as your studio apartment. Your hours may be long. The rewards will depend on your employer. But if you did your homework along the way, you'll know what's in store for you with few surprises.

DON'T THROW OUT YOUR RESUME

The trend now is for people to hold a job for an average of only four years. Career experts say you should constantly be on the outlook for shifts in direction that your company or industry might make as well as changes in your own personal goals. This means always having an updated resume, keeping your skills sharp, and nurturing your network before you need it.

In New York City, you have access like no other to the movers and shakers who shape commerce in this country. Don't wait for your employer to tell you things are going in a different direction. Be proactive. Know where the jobs are in your industry, how the staffing needs of companies are changing, and most importantly, where you fit into it all.

For Your Reference

The other chapters in this book are chock-full of job-search resources, but we've collected some additional ones here for your convenience.

Job Search Assistance

New York State Department of Labor (www.labor.state.ny.us)

Five O'Clock Club (www.fiveoclockclub.com)

Career Research Resources

Job Information Center
Mid-Manhattan Library, 2nd floor
455 Fifth Avenue at 40th Street
New York, NY 10016
212-340-0836
mmjobinf@nypl.org

Science, Technology, and Business Research Library
188 Madison Avenue
New York, NY 10016
212-592-7000

Unemployment Offices

New York State Department of Labor, Division of Employment Services

215 West 125th Street
New York, NY 10027
Phone: 917-493-7200

247 West 54th Street
New York, NY 10019
Phone: 212-621-0701
Fax: 212-621-0435

WetFeet Resources

JOB SEARCH GUIDES

Finding the Right Career Path

Negotiating Your Salary and Perks

Networking Works!

RESUME GUIDES

Killer Consulting Resumes!

Killer Cover Letters and Resumes!

Killer Investment Banking Resumes!

INTERVIEW GUIDES

Ace Your Case!® series for consulting interviews

Ace Your Interview!

Beat the Street® series for investment banking interviews

All WetFeet books available at www.wetfeet.com.

WETFEET'S INSIDER GUIDE SERIES

Job Search Guides

Be Your Own Boss

Changing Course, Changing Careers

Finding the Right Career Path

Getting Your Ideal Internship

International MBA Student's Guide to the U.S. Job Search

Job Hunting A to Z: Landing the Job You Want

Killer Consulting Resumes!

Killer Cover Letters & Resumes!

Killer Investment Banking Resumes!

Negotiating Your Salary & Perks

Networking Works!

Interview Guides

Ace Your Case®: Consulting Interviews

Ace Your Case® II: 15 More Consulting Cases

Ace Your Case® III: Practice Makes Perfect

Ace Your Case® IV: The Latest & Greatest

Ace Your Case® V: Return to the Case Interview

Ace Your Case® VI: Mastering the Case Interview

Ace Your Interview!

Beat the Street®: Investment Banking Interviews

Beat the Street® II: I-Banking Interview Practice Guide

Career & Industry Guides

Careers in Accounting

Careers in Advertising & Public Relations

Careers in Asset Management & Retail Brokerage

Careers in Biotech & Pharmaceuticals

Careers in Brand Management

Careers in Consumer Products

Careers in Entertainment & Sports

Careers in Health Care

Careers in Human Resources

Careers in Information Technology

Careers in Investment Banking

Careers in Management Consulting

Careers in Marketing & Market Research

Careers in Nonprofits & Government Agencies

Careers in Real Estate

Careers in Retail

Careers in Sales

Careers in Supply Chain Management

Careers in Venture Capital

Industries & Careers for MBAs

Industries & Careers for Undergrads

Million-Dollar Careers

Specialized Consulting Careers: Health Care, Human Resources, and Information Technology

Company Guides

25 Top Consulting Firms

25 Top Financial Services Firms

Accenture

Bain & Company

Booz Allen Hamilton

Boston Consulting Group

Credit Suisse First Boston

Deloitte Consulting

Deutsche Bank

The Goldman Sachs Group

J.P. Morgan Chase & Co.

McKinsey & Company

Merrill Lynch & Co.

Morgan Stanley

UBS AG

WetFeet in the City Guides

Job Hunting in New York City

Job Hunting in San Francisco